# SEAMANSHIP IN SMALL
# OPEN BOATS

Also by Ken Duxbury

DINGHY SAILING

# SEAMANSHIP IN SMALL OPEN BOATS

## _Ken Duxbury_

**With illustrations by
the Author**

**PELHAM BOOKS**

First published in Great Britain by
PELHAM BOOKS LTD.,
52, Bedford Square,
London w.c.i
1971

7207 0479 0

Printed in Great Britain by
Western Printing Services, Bristol
in Ten on Twelve Point Caledonia
and bound by James Burn, Esher

# Contents

# Contents

# List of Illustrations

## *Photographs*

## *Drawings*

## List of Illustrations

## List of Illustrations

# Acknowledgements

To John Watts of Rock I present my thanks for many breathless rushes up a windy hillside to obtain the excellent cover photograph and the two sandbar photographs in Chapter One, also for the photos of knots, splices and navigational gear.

My thanks are due also to Duncan Andrew who, as with my first book, again helped to evaporate much fog in the weather section.

Acknowledgement is made to John L. Watkinson, designer of the Drascombe Lugger for the line drawing of that boat, and to Hawkbridge Ltd. of Chichester for the lines of the 'T.24' cruiser. To Dell Quay Ltd. of Chichester for the lines of the 'Fisherboat', and to Fairey Marine Ltd. of Hamble for the superb photo of their 'Spearfish' at speed. The Royal National Lifeboat Institution kindly supplied the photo of their new self-righting 'Solent' class lifeboat undergoing tests.

Lastly I thank my wife who not only valiantly crewed the lugger throughout our two-month voyage, but spent roughly an equal period afterwards sorting, sifting, and finally typing the whole book.

Some crew!

# Note

In order to gain full advantage from Chapters Six, 'Navigation in Small Open Boats' and Chapter Seven, 'The Cruise' the reader is strongly recommended to obtain Admiralty Chart No. 2565 (Trevose Head to Dodman Point, including The Scilly Isles). This can be obtained from any Admiralty Chart Agent.

# Preface

The event which follows took place twelve years ago in a North Cornish estuary. Every detail of that afternoon and evening is clear in my memory, and when you know what happened, we will discuss why and whose fault it was.

Like many shallow estuaries this one has a sandbar across its mouth. It probes into the land from North to South and the wind —brisk from the North West—was enough to make dinghy sailing interesting. The tide was high and just turning to the ebb.

An acquaintance who had been crewing for me the previous week called to ask if he and a friend could borrow or hire my twelve foot sailing dinghy for a couple of hours. I knew the man well enough to be satisfied that he could handle the boat and noted that he had a teen-age boy with him as crew, so readily agreed, remarking that he knew where to find the lifejackets and the boat. I added that he had better have her back on the beach by dusk and keep well up the estuary since the tide had already turned to the ebb.

Ten minutes later I strolled down to the beach to see that all was well. I was never entirely happy when my boat—a typical gunter rigged clinker craft with metal centreplate—was out unattended. True, there were plenty of other craft on the water but I liked to keep an eye on my own property.

They had just got afloat, and were footing it away from shore on a reach, but with misgiving I saw that neither was wearing any form of buoyancy aid. I felt sure that they would have these in the boat with them, but just to check I went to the shed where the boat's gear was kept. The lifejackets were still on their hooks.

This annoyed me. Returning to the beach I saw what gave me my first reason for real concern: despite my advice they were beating down toward the mouth of the estuary and even from where I stood I could see that with the turn of the tide against the wind a wet 'chop' was developing. What is more, an enormous swell was rolling in from sea and I knew that before long, as the tide fell, that swell would start breaking on the bar.

I watched, assuring myself that at any moment the boat would free off the wind and commence running back against the tidal stream toward the safe upper reaches of the estuary. She continued to beat very competently out toward the bar.

By now I was alarmed. I knew the boat, and he knew the boat, and if she was taken much farther to seaward she might well become difficult to handle in the choppy water and even founder. In any case, just up tide of a notoriously dangerous bar is no place to be in a small open dinghy. She continued to beat out to where a white line was occasionally giving an obvious warning that the bar was already showing its teeth.

Surely, I tried to reassure myself, the idiot MUST either bring her on to the beach now, or start running back! Out there the wind was brisker than where I stood watching through the binoculars and already it was clear that the boat was labouring. He approached once more close to the estuary bank, tacked again and headed straight out for the breakers.

By now I was sure I had a couple of suicides on my hands. The moment to act had arrived. I footed it back to the shed for the lifejackets, calling to a friend whose boat I used as a rescue launch to come and help get the boat out to them as quickly as possible. By the time we were clear of the beach and headed full throttle for the bar there was no sail to be seen, nor was my boat beached on either shore. My heart sank.

Before long we had to throttle back ourselves for the sea was too choppy to take the launch at full throttle, and it was then that I saw a glint of light on a varnished upturned hull—just up tide of the line of breakers. A hand was waving. . .

In normal circumstances it would have been criminally foolish to take a small launch just up tide of that area where really large breakers were now appearing fairly regularly. But we had to go. It was really life or death for those two in the water. We HAD to get them aboard at first attempt or they would be into the breakers and we could not follow. That might well mean tragedy, for to drift slowly through two hundred yards or so of big breaking waves is dangerous enough even with a lifejacket on. Without one...?

Until one actually has to carry out a rescue in those conditions it's very hard to appreciate the difficulties. It may well seem to an inexperienced person just a matter of taking the power launch up to the capsized dinghy, scooping the crew aboard, then setting course for home. It's not that easy!

The man had become separated from the boat which was just awash. He was floundering about twenty feet away looking fairly scared. The boy was still clinging to the boat and there was quite a sea running; in fact his head was as much under water as above it. I threw a lifejacket to the boy, bellowing at him to stay with the boat and manoeuvred the launch toward the man.

An approach by boat to a person in choppy water has to be made with extreme caution, for the boat may easily be lifted by a wave and smash down on to the victim's head while getting alongside him. In addition, it is all too easy for him to be run down and severely injured by the propeller. I tied a lifejacket to the end of a line and threw it toward him but the wind took it and carried it a few feet from him. He made no effort to get to the jacket and in fact he was looking very white and frightened with the odd wave breaking over his face.

We got the boat right up to him and dragged him bodily aboard but it took valuable seconds and we were all the time drifting toward the really dangerous area of the bar. A nasty sea slammed against the transom cutting the outboard motor dead. It started—thank Heaven—first pull with the cord otherwise we'd all have gone through that bar together!

Now to try actually to bring the launch alongside the swamped dinghy would have been foolish, for by this time the seas were really building up and we were right in them, on the up tide edge of the bar. The boat might well have been holed, or have crushed the boy between the two craft. Lying a few feet clear to leeward I threw him the line with the lifejacket attached and when he had firm hold of this we pulled him clear of the dinghy and dragged him into the launch. Neither of them could stand.

I can still hear the thunder of those breakers behind us as we headed back up the estuary. The dinghy was recovered by a fisherman later that evening from out at sea in a badly mauled condition, and it cost good money to replace the mast and sails and repair the damage to the hull done by the heavy metal plate which had unshipped completely from its casing.

But it might . . . Ah! It so easily MICHT have been a case of two or even four missing people being searched for by the lifeboat, with the whole train of tragic events following.

Now, WHY did it happen?

The responsibility for the whole affair taking place was mine. It was my boat. It was with my permission that she was taken off the beach and I should have ensured that they were wearing personal buoyancy aids or lifejackets and knew exactly where the dangerous areas lay in the estuary. I knew the man was competent to handle the dinghy: what I misjudged was his common sense. I assumed, quite wrongly, that what would have been obvious to an experienced seaman would also be obvious to a novice.

That man just did not know that a twelve foot open dinghy was not capable of going to sea in such conditions and it eventually turned out that he did not even know the bar existed! To him a boat was a boat, and boats were for going to sea in just as cars were for driving along a road. It was as simple as that, and in fact there is an idiot sort of logic in the approach.

It was of course an extreme example of foolishness and I'm not suggesting for a moment that nine out of ten novices would not have instinctively sensed danger in such a situation. But it did bring home to me the risk of assuming that seamanship—and by that I mean the vast wealth of background knowledge and experience pertaining to every aspect of boat handling at sea—is just a part of common sense; sense, that is, which is common to all. In fact, it was really as a result of that event twelve years ago that the concept of this book was born.

Today, with the tremendous explosion in popularity of dinghies and small boats, more and more of us are tending to 'pop outside' the shelter of our home waters for the day cruise down a coast. Indeed, many of us do not have the luxury of sheltered harbours and estuaries, but launch straight from the beach to the open sea.

It is here that certain new hazards begin to rear their heads of which the part-time small boat operator may not even be aware.

Whether you gingerly lower yourself into a twelve foot kayak on the rippled edge of a beach, or point the proud bows of a luxury cruiser seaward, you OUGHT to know something about the game. Experience itself cannot of course be passed on . . . it literally must happen to you before you count it experience . . . but the knowledge of what might happen, and how to set about avoiding it, or coping with it when it DOES happen, CAN be passed on.

That is the object of this book.

# 1

# Wind and Water

Sometimes the question is put to me, 'Would this be a safe boat in which to go . . .' well, it matters not—across the Atlantic, the Channel or the duckpond. I tend to bristle.

Far more to the point in my opinion would be the question, 'Am I a safe person to take this boat across. . . .' Of course, the truth of the matter, so far as safety is concerned, is that both boat and crew have to be adequate for the job. The *Queen Elizabeth* within twenty yards of the dockside in calm water could be a frightful hazard if handled by a chump. On the other hand a sixteen foot sailing dinghy ten miles off shore when in the charge of a skilled seaman could be as safe as the Bank of England. Or perhaps safer.

The reason is quite simple. The chap in the dinghy would know the elements he's dealing with—wind and water—the limitations of his boat, and his own capabilities to cope with whatever situations arose. What is just as important, excepting the arrival of the most unusual bad luck, he would be sure that nothing he was unable to cope with was looming up. If it was, he would not be there!

This is what seamanship is about, and I have chosen its application to really small boats as the subject of this book because it is in such boats that one is truly 'in touch' with the elements. At risk of being taken too literally, I will state that the larger one's craft the more one can afford to ignore certain aspects of the sea and weather. Their hour-by-hour and sometimes minute-by-minute changes of mood are, however, in a small boat, of vital importance calling for immediate decisions. The safety margin is too narrow for them to be ignored.

This is what makes the whole game worthwhile, and the more you know about it the more satisfying it becomes.

So let us start by surveying the arena: wind and water. We will think about their interaction upon one another, then take a look at how this interaction itself is affected by the environ—lake, river, estuary or open sea.

### THE EFFECT OF WIND ON WATER

When moving air comes into contact with water, surface friction results which is simply a transfer of energy from the one medium to the other, and sooner or later this manifests itself in wave form. This wave formation will grow under the continued influence of a steady wind and produce a more or less regular surface pattern which a sailor refers to as 'sea'.

Where a large storm with high winds is centred above a vast area of water, the waves so formed will continue out and away from the relatively localised centre of their origin, and after travelling perhaps hundreds of miles—sometimes with no wind affecting them whatever—will be detectable as long, low and fairly regular undulations which are then known as 'swell'. Drop a stone in a pond and watch the ripples. You will see this effect in miniature.

In due course, other winds—often blowing in the opposite or cross direction to that in which the swell is advancing—will form another sea pattern superimposed on this swell, perhaps almost concealing its presence under the shorter contrary or cross travelling waves.

But when the swell, having arrived at the edges of an ocean or sea, begins to feel the bottom in shallowing water, three things happen. First, its rate of advance begins to slow up almost as if it were feeling an effect of a brake down there underneath. Secondly and simultaneously, these wave crests begin to rear up higher and become narrower while the trough between them deepens and the distance from wave crest to wave crest starts to become shorter, i.e. its 'wave length' becomes less. Can you visualise the effect? Figure 1 will help.

What started, perhaps to an observer on a high cliff, as a perceptible long, low and fast-moving undulation out at sea, tends, as it advances across the shallowing water off the shoreline, to slow down in its advance and 'concertina' as it does so, the crests becoming much more pronounced and closer together. An acute observer will notice however that this slowing down of the advancing waves is exactly balanced by a shortening of the wave length, so that the time intervals at which the crests and troughs

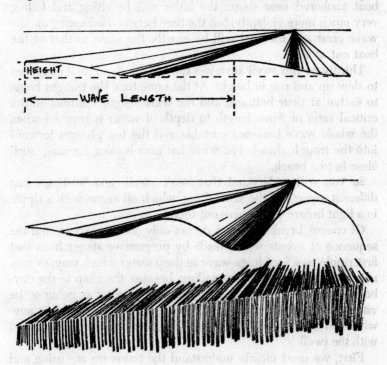

*Figure 1   Wave formation*

*Top:*
*A wave in deep water showing the method of measuring its height and wave length. The period of a wave is the time interval between one crest passing a fixed point and the next adjacent crest passing the same point.*

*Bottom:*
*The effect of shallowing water on a wave. Speed of advance slows. Wave length shortens. Period remains the same. Height of crest increases.*

pass a fixed point remain the same. In other words, their 'period' remains constant.

You can check this in the right conditions by watching a small fishing boat lying at its nets near the horizon and timing its 'rise and fall' out in the long undulations. Compare this with another boat anchored near shore: the latter will be rising and falling very much more violently, but the time between balancing on one wave crest and the next will be exactly the same as that of the boat out at sea.

Thirdly, as this swell advances toward the shore, so it continues to slow up and rise in height. At the same time the troughs begin to flatten at their bottoms, and the wave length shortens until a critical ratio of wave length to depth of water is reached when the whole wave becomes unstable and the top plunges forward into the trough ahead. The wave has now broken, forming 'surf' close in to a beach.

So you will understand that 'sea', 'swell' and 'surf' are just different aspects of the same thing, which all began with a ripple in a light breeze somewhere out there!

Of course, breaking waves do not only occur on shore, and the sequence of events which leads by progressive stages from that first ripple to a final huge wave in deep water which may, or may not, break, is worth understanding, because the chap in the day-boat who decides to take a trip along the coast is going to be vitally concerned with the sea, and if he proposes landing any-where on an exposed beach, should most certainly be concerned with the swell.

First, we must clearly understand the terms we are using and Figure 1 will again help. The 'wave length' is the distance from the top of one crest to the next. The wave 'height' is the vertical distance from the top of the crest to the bottom of the trough. The wave 'velocity' is the rate of travel of a wave in a horizontal direction and the wave 'period' is the interval of time between one wave crest passing a fixed point and the succeeding wave crest passing that same fixed point.

Starting then from the beginning, imagine the ocean to be calm as a pond. Now a light wind fans across its surface forming ripples. Each ripple presents more resistance to the wind on its 'weather' side than on its 'lee' side and by this effect more energy is transferred from wind to wave. The wave gets bigger. This effect is not completely regular—some waves are higher than their brothers—and gradually the larger waves tend to get larger still, increasing in both length and height, the former being at this stage about thirteen times the value of the latter.

You may be wondering whether the formation and augmentation of these waves by the wind can go on indefinitely to result in ever increasing wave sizes. This might appear logical only if we overlook the fact that the size of the wave formed must be related to the strength and duration of the wind acting on it. In fact, the size of a wave is an indication of the energy it contains, and it cannot carry on absorbing energy from the wind if the wind has no more energy to give!

Until that state of balance is reached, however, one of the important factors governing the size of a wave is the expanse of water across which the wind is free to blow. This latter is called the 'fetch' and it will be obvious that, regardless of depth, the formation (if any) of waves across a gully of water one yard wide will be very different from those waves formed by the same wind blowing across a mile of water. Do you get the picture? Given a large enough fetch of deep water, the maximum size of a wave formed is entirely dependent on the velocity of the wind and the duration. After that maximum size is reached, the wave will not increase in size unless the wind strengthens or the duration lengthens.

So you see there is a theoretical limit, with any given wind strength and duration and fetch to the size of a wave which can form, but the sea (thank Heaven!) has a splendid time confounding theories. For instance, if waves happen to be emanating from two different areas of one large storm centre—or better still from two separate storm centres—when they meet and cross one another they often 'build up' as it were on to one another's backs to form freaks of very different size and shape.

It can work the other way round too: if two converging areas of waves have a slightly different period, they will tend to build up and then cancel out their respective wave forms, as they alternately get 'in step' and 'out of step' so to speak.

This results in areas of big waves followed by areas with almost no waves at all, and any bather on a beach will have experienced it. The big ones sometimes catch you unaware after that 'lull' period!

Back to deep water. What is happening to the water itself, as this wave form undulates across its surface? The best thing we can do is to float a cork on the surface of the water and imagine ourselves to be looking at it through the side of a vast aquarium window so that we are free to see the movement of the cork up and down, forward and backward, and also—this is important—we can put a mark on the glass to act as a fixed reference point against which we can relate the amount of movement of the cork. See Figure 2.

Along comes a succession of waves. Select one—anyone will do. As it approaches, the cork will commence to drop and move back toward the trough just ahead of the wave and it will be at its lowest point and moving at maximum speed back toward the advancing wave when slap in the centre of the trough—halfway between two waves. From that point on it will begin to rise, slowing in its backward movement as it does so until halfway up the advancing face where it will stop its backward motion and while still rising commence to move forward. When right on top of the crest it will be moving forward at its maximum speed, to progressively reduce that speed as it commences to drop down the back of the wave until, halfway down, it has lost all forward motion and again commences to swing back into the next trough.

If we had marked on the surface of the glass the exact movement of that cork we would have traced a circle. The next time the cork traced out a circle with the passage of the next complete wave cycle, it would do so apparently in the same place on the glass, because the water in which it is floating is not itself advancing with the waves—at least very very little. There is a slight advance: but it amounts to a mere one per cent or thereabouts of the wave velocity.

So much for a cork floating on the surface, and you will have realised that the diameter of that circle it has just swung around is equal to the wave height.

But what about the water under the surface? Carry out an experiment: arrange that some object remains in free suspension beneath the surface at a depth equal to about one quarter of the wave length. You will find, as the wave passes, that it still de-

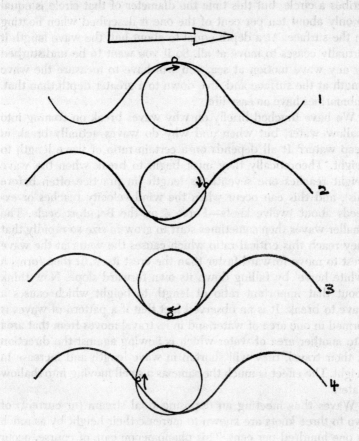

*Figure 2*

*Orbital Motion of a particle of water as a wave passes.*
*(At surface)*

**Arrow at top shows direction of wave travel. Cork represents**
*particle.*

1. *Cork on crest moving fast to right.*
2. *Cork plunging downward on back of wave.*
3. *Cork in trough moving backward fast.*
4. *Cork rising upward on front of wave.*

27

scribes a circle, but this time the diameter of that circle is equal to only about ten per cent of the one it described when floating on the surface. At a depth equal to about half the wave length it virtually ceases to move at all. So if you want to be undisturbed by any wave motion at sea, you will have to measure the wave length at the surface and dive down to a greater depth than that. Submarines have an easy life.

We have touched briefly on why waves break on coming into shallow water, but when and why do waves actually break in deep water? It all depends on a certain ratio of wave length to height. Theoretically they must begin to break when the wave height reaches one seventh its length (in practice often before this), and this can occur when the wind velocity reaches or exceeds about twelve knots—Force 4 on the Beaufort Scale. The smaller waves then sometimes start to grow in size so rapidly that they reach this critical ratio which causes the water at the wave crest to move forward faster than the crest itself. It then forms a 'white horse' by falling down its own forward slope. Now think about that important ratio of length to height which causes a wave to break. It is an observed fact that if a pattern of waves is formed in one area of water and in its travel moves from that area into another area of water which is flowing against the direction of their travel, they will shorten in wave length and increase in height. The effect is much the same as a swell moving into shallow water.

Waves thus meeting an opposing tidal stream (or current) of two to three knots are known to increase their height by as much as one hundred per cent. This phenomenon can, of course, occur when a contra-running tidal stream starts to flow, or changes direction. Waves already generated by the wind may be just below the breaking point, and on feeling the adverse effect of the changed tidal stream plus the relatively increased strength of the wind (if any) will shorten up and start to break.

It is important to remember this if you find yourself in a situation where tidal stream and wind are in the same direction and the seas have reached that stage where they are not quite breaking. You may be sure that with the change of the tidal stream they will do so: it matters in a small boat. Don't be caught out.

Now let us consider these wind and water reactions in their

different environs, namely lakes, rivers, estuaries and the open sea, with an eye on our man in the open dayboat.

## LAKES

Big or small, these will be inland areas of water and therefore not able to respond to the tide-raising forces of sun and moon, so in that respect the boat handler has one less thing to bear in mind. From the safety point of view of course one can drown just as easily in a pond as in the middle of the Pacific given the wrong circumstances, such as a severe blow on the head to help the process, or just an inability to swim.

But on average dangers to life and limb are not quite as likely to arise in lakes as in the more unprotected areas of water. Long exposure while clinging to an upturned boat is possible on a lake but must be a very rare occurrence. If there is any wind you are almost certain to have a shore not too far down to leeward on to which you will be gently drifting, and the size of the waves, even on a biggish deep lake are not likely to physically wrench you away from your boat, or even preclude adequate breathing if you do get separated, provided you are wearing a lifejacket or buoyancy aid. And since no swell can ever develop in a lake, when you finally reach the shore you will not be pulverised!

The important thing is that your boat—whatever it may be— must be either so inherently stable as to be virtually uncapsizable, or if it relies on acrobatic skill such as a fast racing dinghy, it must be unsinkable. I mean unsinkable: lying on its beam or turned turtle it should still form a useful platform on which you and your crew can sit indefinitely until either you drift ashore or are rescued or can get the craft sailing again. This is common sense, and applies to any boat on any water, but it is, alas, all too often overlooked by failure to periodically check the watertightness of hatches to built-in buoyancy compartments, or the adequacy of the lashings on tied-in buoyancy bags.

Provided you and the boat will continue to float, even though your motive power has gone, on a lake you are fairly safe.

## RIVERS

There are rivers, of course, *and* rivers. The meadow-flanked willow-studded brand have far more beauty value than built-in hazards, and anyone who comes to grief on such a stretch of water is either exceptionally unlucky or exceptionally foolish.

The larger sort, which allow more unrestricted use by boats, can present very real hazards. The obvious fact that they flow downhill toward the sea can provide exciting incidents, and I have been up the Rhone and down the Garonne in conditions which would have been lunatic for a small open boat, with high wind against a turbulent current literally boiling and swirling with nasty steep short waves superimposed. To be pitched into that sort of current may result in a really dangerous situation. Not primarily because the strong current is taking one along—it will be taking the boat or any other floating object along as well so that relative to the water all is motionless: the danger lies in the violent underwater turbulence which can very easily submerge a man, or for that matter a waterlogged boat.

It is a common misconception that 'the current took him away from the boat'. It does nothing of the sort unless the boat is anchored to the bottom in which case it certainly will remove you from the boat—and fast if you once become separated!

Wind tends to be more chancy on a river where surrounding hills and trees have a very local effect, and this is a splendid challenge to the dinghy sailor.

But generally the surface conditions will, in a high wind, be similar to those experienced in any shallow water with a short fetch. Lakes and rivers, however, while calling for certain obvious precautions which apply to any boat anywhere, do not strictly call for the exercise of seamanship in its wider sense. This is not the case with estuaries.

ESTUARIES

Here we have the influence of the open sea and its strong tidal effects. The winds, too, which affect estuaries are likely to be meeting their first hindrance in the form of land after passing across hundreds or even a thousand miles or so of open water. This can make for really exhilarating sailing and bouncy high-speed launch work. Surface conditions change noticeably depending on whether it is High or Low Water. Around High Water, when there is some depth, a sizeable short steep chop can soon develop, particularly if the wind is blowing against the tidal stream. Overfalls—that turbulence caused by water swirling round a prominence or boiling over a sudden shallow patch of the seabed—can turn this short steep sea into a confused and exciting piece of water for the small dayboat. I have myself been swamped in a twelve foot sailing dinghy well up an estuary due simply to driving her too hard into the short steep waves caused by the wind blowing against the tidal stream.

With the change of the tidal stream, conditions can alter almost beyond recognition: what was an exhilarating stretch of water may become a quite placid flow with an apparently much reduced wind speed if you're out there in a boat. In fact, it may well be that the wind is just as brisk as ever, but now, by virtue of the change of tide, it is blowing in the same direction as the tidal stream so that the relative wind speed is reduced greatly, making the sailing somewhat tame.

This is the playground of the small powerboats and sailing dinghies, often nipping about between their larger sisters, the coastal cruisers and off shore yachts. The seaworthiness of the craft must be suited, and so must the competence of those who use them.

It is tempting to embark on advice as to exactly which type of craft is best suited to an estuary but the variety is so great that one tends to get bogged down in contradictions and qualifications of any statement. For instance, sailing dinghies with 'planing' hulls which literally water ski across the surface are frequently used by acrobats in hair-raising conditions on estuaries. One might pose the question, 'Are such craft really boats? Or would they better be labelled aquatic racing machines!' The point is that in one most important respect they do fulfil the basic requirement of any boat: they will not sink. Swamp them, roll them over and sit three hefty chaps on their undersides while the mast breaks off short on the seabed—they will remain buoyant and support the crew safely for an indefinite time. Which is more than can be said for a good number of the 'traditional' craft which are generally considered to be seaworthy boats.

The size of the waves which can be whipped up by a wind on an estuary can certainly cause severe damage to a boat which may be left in a waterlogged state on the lee shore. Remember that water is some six hundred times denser than air, and if allowed to get a good grip on anything, can wreak fearful havoc. Indeed, as you get into this book you may come to realise that the art lies in not allowing the sea to get to grips with your boat any more than is absolutely necessary! However, as on a lake, waves in an estuary are unlikely ever to actually endanger life and limb even in the most ridiculous situation.

The real hazard in shallow estuaries is the mouth, where it meets the sea. In almost all wide shallow estuaries there is a deposit of sand across the entrance which forms what is in effect a submerged beach called a 'bar'. Just as waves break on a beach, so the larger waves will break on this submerged beach IF THE TIDE IS LOW ENOUGH.

This is where experience—local experience—is essential. It is not just a case of observing what is happening on the sand bar at the moment when you look at it. It is knowing what is going to or likely to happen, in the immediate future. The event described in the preface is a typical example of what can happen through ignorance: that chap was quite unaware that the bar was becoming a real danger to a small boat, and since estuaries form one of the largest playgrounds for all types of small craft it will pay us to take a good look at this sand bar phenomenon.

The situation on a bar such as we are thinking about depends on two things: the size and direction of the swell which is rolling in from sea, and the depth of water on the bar—i.e. the state of the tide.

We will look at a typical sequence of events, assuming it is Low Water and a moderate swell is rolling in from sea with little wind. At first, the breakers will probably be continuous right across the estuary mouth. The depth of water over the bar may vary from a foot or two at one end to perhaps six or ten feet at the other—one end is generally deeper than the other—but we will assume that the swell is large enough to break right the way across. This line of breakers will be fairly accurately defining the outer limit of the sand bar, and entry or exit of the estuary would be barred to all craft.

As the tide rises, the tidal stream begins to flow into the estuary. The line of breakers will tend to advance slowly into the mouth, since the point at which they start breaking, in terms of depth, is receding gradually up the estuary. As the tide continues to rise so the pattern of breakers on the bar will change. The shallow end will continuously break as before, but tend to extend over a larger area farther into the mouth, while the deeper end will begin to break only intermittently. But these intermittent breakers will be the big ones.

With the increasing depth as the tide rises, sooner or later the deep end ceases to break altogether, although there may still be unbroken swell rearing up ominously before it finally subsides without actually breaking. At the shallow end the breakers will tend to move farther and farther into the mouth until breaking only at the shallowest ridge of the bar and becoming more intermittent but larger. Finally, when the tide is perhaps just after half flood—halfway to High Water—they will cease to break altogether. From now on the bar is safe to cross in a small boat, other conditions permitting.

At High Water you may not appreciate that there is a bar there at all. The large swells rolling in from sea may rear up a little and become noticeable to a chap passing over the bar, but their energy is gradually dispersed, and shows itself probably in nothing more than a marked 'surge' up and down the beaches farther up the estuary.

As the tide begins to fall and the tidal stream flows out of the mouth, so the real hazard to boats starts again. It is from now on that boats should stay well up the higher reaches of an estuary and not under any circumstances put themselves in a position where a power failure—wind or motor—can result in them going over the bar with the outward flowing stream.

More or less the reverse process takes place with regard to the breakers, but generally it all happens farther out of the mouth, more to seaward, and in the more pronounced form we would expect from our understanding of wave formations. The outflowing stream inhibits the tendency to break inside the estuary as the tide falls, but on reaching the advancing swell from seaward makes it build up into a nasty steep wave formation at the shallow end near the mouth and then progressively more across the entrance until once again the whole mouth is a line of white, with the bigger breakers tending toward the deeper end.

The photographs in Plate 1 were taken at the entrance to the Camel Estuary in North Cornwall, when a light Westerly wind was blowing across the estuary mouth. The top photo shows Low Water Spring Tide with the breakers forming right across the seaward edge of the sand bar. Some idea of relative size may be gained by the man standing at the centre of the beach. The lower photo was taken three hours later at half tide when the depth had increased some eight feet. Already, due to the increased depth, the swell had ceased to break at the left hand shallow end of the estuary mouth and had in fact moved in to break just out of the left hand edge of the photo farther into the mouth. I was thinking at the time that all activity at the mouth had ceased but that creamer shown in the lower photo suddenly broke out in deep water. This wave does not look much in the photo: waves seldom do, but it was quite large enough to 'pitchpole' (turn end-over-end) a fourteen-foot dinghy or small power launch had they been caught in it. One can never quite predict where these unexpected last breakers are going to appear.

With regard to the actual danger to boats, this falls into two categories. The obvious chance of swamping or capsize in the breakers applies to the smaller craft, and believe me the wave is always a much more formidable opponent when you're in it than it appears from a distance. If you're lucky, you may enjoy the experience—afterwards! For the bigger boats—perhaps twenty feet to forty feet in length with good freeboard, it may well be that they can cope with the actual breaker. What they have to guard against is striking the bottom in the troughs. Down at that deeper end of the bar, at Low Water, the mean depth may be around six to ten feet where the big ones are humping up and occasionally breaking. You have only to hit the bottom once, when the craft is plunging down in a trough and that is enough! It is very unlikely, however, to be only once. If you hit at all, the chances are that you will hit three or four times before you are clear of the bar. It does a boat no good at all.

Of course, the precise activity on a bar depends on many factors—the shape of the sand bar, which is governed chiefly by the configuration of the estuary banks and the type and shape of the coast immediately to seaward at both sides. The direction from which the swell is rolling in has a great influence also, as does the exact state of the tidal stream both inside and outside the estuary. However, the above example applies to a fairly

34

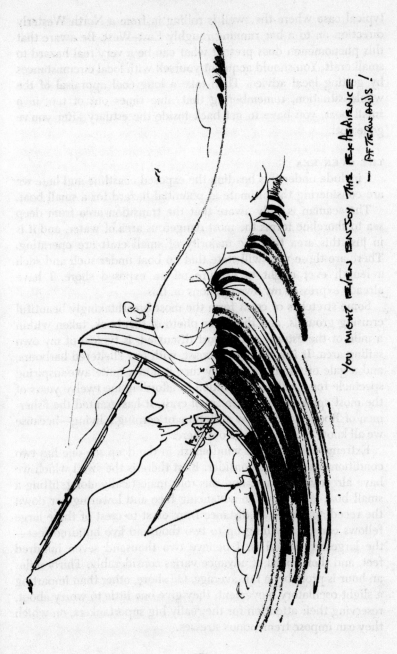

typical case where the swell is rolling in from a North Westerly direction on to a bar running roughly East–West. Be aware that this phenomenon does present what can be a very real hazard to small craft. You should acquaint yourself with local circumstances by getting local advice. Then take a long cool appraisal of the whole situation, remembering that nine times out of ten, in a small boat, you have to get back inside the estuary after you've gone out!

### THE OPEN SEA

I include under this heading the exposed coastline and here we are considering the ultimate in potential hazard for a small boat.

The seaman is fully aware that the transition area from deep sea to shoreline forms the most dangerous area of water, and it is in just this area that the majority of small craft are operating. There are those who will state that no boat under such and such a length ever ought to venture off an exposed shore. I have already expressed my own opinions on this.

Some stretches of coast form the most breathtakingly beautiful cruising grounds, and the cover photo of this book, taken within a mile of the estuary mouth just discussed, is typical of my own sailing area. It is a dangerous coast, with few sheltered harbours, and a gale of wind can quickly turn it into a quite awe-inspiring spectacle for a sailor. In addition to affording me twelve years of the most splendid sailing in small craft, it has granted the fishermen of Rock and Padstow a lifetime of earning a living—because we all know when NOT to be out there.

Extreme conditions of wind apart, in the deep sea one has two conditions of water to consider. First there is the swell which we have already discussed, and this rolls majestically along, lifting a small boat gently up the advancing face and lowering her down the receding face. The distance from crest to crest of these large fellows can be anything up to two thousand five hundred feet— the largest recorded is, I believe two thousand seven hundred feet, and their speed of advance varies considerably. Thirty miles an hour is probably a fair average. Off shore, other than imparting a slight oscillatory movement, they give one little to worry about, reserving their attention for the really big supertankers, on which they can impose tremendous stresses.

The second surface condition—the one all smaller boats are vitally concerned with—is the 'sea' caused by the immediate wind. This can, in deep water, reach proportions that preclude survival of a small dayboat with an open cockpit. Granted that the boat may have built-in buoyancy tanks quite adequate to keep her floating in a swamped or capsized condition, the crew will nevertheless be more or less subjected to an onslaught of water, probably breaking over the boat in the form of large 'white horses' for many hours without cease. Exposure soon weakens a person in such conditions, and just for the lack of a comparatively dry cabin where even in extreme discomfort one can keep warm and snatch something to eat—the end of the affair can be disaster. The open sea, well off shore, is not for ninety-nine per cent of small boat users. The odd one per cent who do undertake epic voyages in dayboats are exceptional not only in their seamanship but in every other respect as well. I take my hat off to them.

As one approaches the coast, two additional hazards may present themselves. Firstly the big swell which could be disregarded in deep water begins to feel the bottom. As it rolls in over the shallowing sea—probably miles out from shore—it will begin to follow the inevitable pattern, heaping up and greatly increasing the height from trough to crest. It may be that if the shallowing water extends over a sufficiently large area, the energy which these big fellows carry along with them in wave form will be gradually dispersed before they ever reach the stage of breakdown, but they have only to meet in their passage a localised shallower patch—and they can be 'tripped up' to crash with frightening power, leaving a tell-tale splurge of white froth far out to sea to mark the shallows. Frequently only one in every dozen or so will break—just the one which is that little bit deeper from trough to crest—and this is what can make these off shore banks so dangerous.

The second hazard is of course the shoreline itself. Here every bit of energy the sea contained, be it lumbering up in the form of a truly massive swell or rippling along in dappled wavelets, is finally and completely dispersed. One inch inside a vertical cliff face, one foot up a sandy beach—the power has gone. Somewhere between deep water and dry land all the latent energy has been released. Thrust, heat, motion or sound, whatever form it takes, the shore will have borne the brunt of it.

This is what makes coastal cruising such a challenge: one is skirting the edge of a battle ground between sea and land. Make no mistake, when the skirmish waxes fierce it's better not to be around!

From my own experience I would say that for some seventy-five per cent of the time I have spent coasting along exposed beaches, landing has been out of the question. Of course, even if there is a big swell and wetting sea running, there is sometimes the odd protected beach in the lee of a headland or at one side of a deep bay, but these hardly come within the category of exposed beaches.

Before leaving this introductory survey of wind and water, it will be useful to take a look at two other reactions of swell when its passage is blocked by islands and beaches.

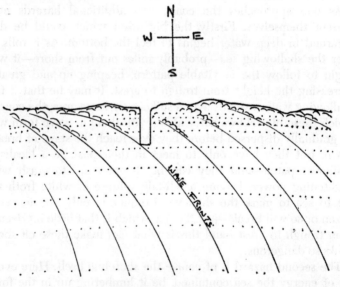

*Figure 3*

*Bending of waves due to refraction on meeting the gradual incline of seabed up to a beach. Breakers may form closer to the East side of that jetty than you expect.*

We have already noted that on approaching shallow water the swell, while retaining its period, slows the speed of its forward advance and shortens the length between crests. You can visualise therefore what happens when a swell is advancing at an angle on to a long shallow beach. Look at Figure 3.

The left hand end of the swells are feeling this slowing-down effect first so a bend has to result along the advancing front of the wave. The pattern illustrated develops, and you can see this very clearly on the right sort of beach in this condition of swell. It is worth remembering because if for any reason you decide to attempt a landing where there is a groyne or perhaps a protruding rock, the shelter which you had expected it to afford from the breakers may not be as great as you expect. This bending phenomenon is called 'refraction'.

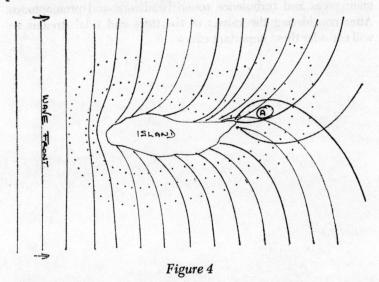

*Figure 4*

*Wave pattern formed by refraction round an island. Sea may be very confused at (A).*

In exactly the same way, refraction of swell advancing towards a small island with shallow surrounds can result in a confused wave form at the far side of the island. Consider Figure 4. The advancing wave fronts are retarded in their contacting edges as they pass down either side of the island, to continue refracting round under the far side, where they meet each other and form a cross pattern which can be very significant to a small boat. One may be seeking shelter from the wind in exactly that position where the sea is confused if it happens that the swell and wind are coming from the same direction. Of course this phenomenon does not occur where the shore is steep-to.

So much for our general survey of the arena. Now we must take a look at another phenomenon of the sea which any sailor should understand: tides and tidal streams. They are of real consequence to the small boat handler in so far as he will need to know not only the depth of water, but the speed and direction of its flow so as to use it to help and not hinder his passage. This latter flow can be the cause of one real danger to a small boat man: races and turbulence round headlands and promontories. After considering the causes of the tides and tidal streams we will consider these important effects.

# 2

# Tides and Weather

## THE CAUSE OF TIDES

Most people are aware that the rise and fall of a tide in the ocean is caused by the gravitational pull of the moon and the sun—chiefly the former—and it would be easy to imagine this 'bulge' in the water as it were being pulled around the earth as she rotates on her axis once in twenty-four hours. This highly idealised concept bears very little resemblance to the observed reactions of our seas to this tide-raising force however.

More probably, if the earth were completely covered by very deep water, there would be not one, but two of these bulges moving round once in every twenty-four hours, and they would be positioned more or less diametrically opposite to one another and caused primarily by the moon. The reason for there being two bulges is fairly easy to understand and throws up a rarely considered fact with regard to the earth-moon system.

We all accept that the moon orbits round the earth in one lunar month but this is not quite the whole story. Disregarding for a moment the rest of the solar system, this earth-moon system is itself orbiting round one common centre of gravity in absolute equilibrium. This common centre of gravity is called the bary-centre and if we take it as our point of reference for a moment and choose to call it 'stationary' in space, we would find that it falls just inside the earth's surface; about a fifth of the way in toward the earth's centre. The earth itself is 'wobbling' around this point while the moon (being much smaller in mass) does most of the moving and orbits around the barycentre well away from it. In doing so it also orbits around the earth.

But the tide raising force (gravity) which, remember, is keeping

41

the whole earth-moon system in equilibrium, is just like a magnet in so far as it acts with greater force on a near object than on an object farther away. It follows that the water on the earth's face nearest to the moon will feel a stronger pull (and respond more) than will water on the earth's face farthest from the moon.

It also follows—and this is the really important bit—that the solid earth between these two areas of water will feel (and respond to) a gravitational force of a value somewhere in between the two we have just been considering. Can you see what happens?

The water nearest to the moon is drawn up into a bulge. The solid earth has to respond to a slightly weaker gravitational pull which is the mean of its whole width. But the water farthest from the moon tends to heap up into a bulge also, because it is responding to an even weaker pull and therefore, as it were, gets left behind. You can think of it as being flung off by centrifugal force from the outer face of the earth-moon orbiting system as it 'wobbles' round that barycentre—it amounts to the same thing.

Exactly the same phenomena would be produced by the sun, though in a much less degree. In fact the sun's tide generating force is not strong enough to produce a tidal response which is appreciable as being separate to that of the stronger moon effect. So in our ideal state therefore there would be just the two reciprocally positioned bulges which represent the top of the wave oscillation. Between them would be the trough which represents the point of low water. Such might be the situation if our globe were completely covered with very deep water. Any point on that rotating globe would therefore experience two periods of High Water and two periods of Low Water in every twenty-four hours.

The surface of our earth however is broken up with irregularly-shaped land masses, and those areas which are covered with water also vary greatly in depth. This completely disrupts the theoretical response of the water we have just been considering. It is an observed fact that the response by way of tides in the different oceans and seas varies greatly, and is very complex, being linked to shape, depth, and position on the earth's surface which gives the different water masses what might be thought of as a 'resonance' which is capable of responding sometimes in harmony with and sometimes almost completely out of harmony with the tide generating forces.

Around the coast of Britain however it is an observed fact that we experience High Water (the top of the bulge) approximately every twelve hours. The advancing bulge—I prefer to call it this rather than 'wave' because of its truly colossal proportions— arrives off the coast of Portugal at Zero plus two hours. At Zero plus three hours it is off the Western coast of France and at Zero plus four hours it arrives off Lands End. Here it divides, part of it going up the English Channel to arrive in the Straits of Dover at Zero plus eleven hours. The other part carries on up the Western coast of Ireland arriving at the Orkneys at about Zero plus nine hours when it sweeps round into the North Sea and undulates down the East coast of England arriving off Peterhead

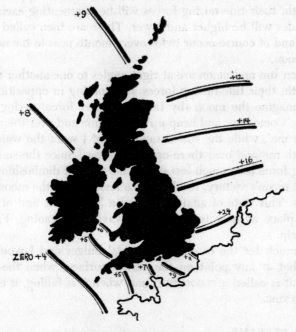

*Figure 5*

*Advance of the Tidal Bulge*
*Around Great Britain*

at Zero plus twelve hours. It continues on down the East coast until, at Zero plus twenty-four hours it is off Harwich where it meets, not its other half from which it originally separated, but that half's successor which started off from somewhere in mid-Atlantic at Zero plus twelve hours and had followed the original bulge up the English Channel while the first bulge was still undulating round the much longer path. Figure 5 shows this pattern.

The size of the bulges—that is the height of the High Water—depends entirely on the position of sun and moon relative to earth. Although as we have noted, the sun's effect is hardly appreciable as a separate tide-raising force, it nevertheless is appreciable as an augmenting or diminishing effect on the tides raised by the moon. Since they are both magnets acting on the free-flowing water it will be evident that when sun and moon are in line with one another either on the same side or opposite sides of earth, their tide-raising forces will be augmenting each other. The tides will be higher and lower. These are then called Spring Tides and of course occur twice every month near to the new and full moon.

When sun and moon are at right angles to one another relative to earth, their tide-raising forces are working in opposition. You may imagine the moon (by far the greater force) saying to the water, 'Come here and heap up beneath me and over there opposite to me', while the sun is saying, 'No! I want the water here beneath me and over there opposite to me.' Since the sun's tide-raising force is so much less it only has a slight diminishing effect on the moon's victory, resulting in a lessening of the moon's tidal bulges. This state of affairs is called a Neap Tide and of course takes place at near to half-moon, waxing or waning. Figure 6 will help.

So much for the causes of the tidal bulges and I would only add that at any point on the earth's surface, when the tide is rising it is called a FLOOD TIDE, and when it is falling, it is called an EBB TIDE.

## TIDAL STREAMS

But now I want you to think of something which is quite different—the horizontal FLOW of water which has to take place in order for these huge tidal bulges to exist.

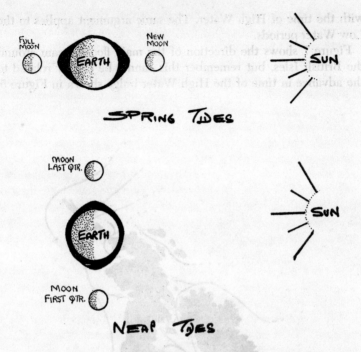

*Figure 6*

*The position of sun and moon in relation to earth at
Spring and Neap tides.*

It will be evident that really vast quantities of water have to
be moved slightly in order that these bulges may be drawn up.
This horizontal flow of water is called a 'tidal stream'.

Frequently the terms 'flood stream' and 'ebb stream' are taken
to imply that the tidal stream flows in one direction while the
tide is flooding (rising) and another (perhaps reciprocal) direction
while the tide is ebbing (falling). This can be very misleading, for
while this is the case in tidal estuaries, it certainly does not apply
out along the coast.

In fact, along a coast the tide can be flooding, reach High Water
and commence to ebb again while all the time the flood stream
flows in one direction. Eventually the flood stream will slacken,
stop, and turn to an ebb stream but it will not necessarily coincide

45

with the time of High Water. The same argument applies to the Low Water periods.

Figure 7 shows the direction of the main flood stream around the British Isles, but remember this cannot be closely related to the advance in time of the High Water bulge shown in Figure 5.

*Figure 7*

*The Main Flood Stream direction round*
*the British Isles*

When referring to a tidal stream along a coastline, rather than use the terms 'ebb stream' and 'flood stream' it is better to refer to the direction of flow such as 'North East going stream' or 'South West going stream'.

Remember that when speaking of tidal streams, unlike a wind, the direction is referred to as that in which the stream is flowing. A North wind blows FROM the North. A Northerly tidal stream flows TOWARD the North.

Lastly, never confuse tidal streams with currents. Currents are one-way only movements of water in the ocean or a river, in the former case caused by a wind perhaps, or different temperatures of water resulting in a convectional flow. It is tempting to confuse these two, but should be avoided in the interests of accuracy. We shall be using these tidal streams to full advantage during the cruise in Chapter 7.

TIDAL DEFINITIONS

When dealing with tidal phenomena it is very important to use the correct terms, and I list below some tidal definitions together with a visual representation of a tide pole. (Figure 8)

CHART DATUM: The level below which depths are shown on the chart. The height of the tide must therefore be added to obtain an actual depth. The tide very seldom falls below Chart Datum.

MEAN SEA LEVEL: The average level of the surface of the sea.

TIDAL OSCILLATION: A tidal wave represents one vertical oscillation about the mean level of the sea. It includes one High and the succeeding Low Water.

HIGH WATER and LOW WATER: The highest and lowest level reached by the surface of the sea in one tidal oscillation.

MEAN HIGH WATER NEAPS and MEAN HIGH WATER SPRINGS: The average heights of High Water Springs and High Water Neaps taken over a long period.

RISE OF THE TIDE: The height of High Water above Chart Datum.

47

EQUINOCTIAL
SPRING TIDES:

The greatest range of tide possible during a year. These occur in March and September when the sun is vertically above our equator. This being the case, sun, moon and earth all lie in the same plane and the tide-raising force is therefore acting on exactly the same point on the earth's surface.

The difference in levels of successive High and Low Waters is called the range of the tide and depends of course on whether the tide is Spring or Neap. At the Port of Bristol the range can,

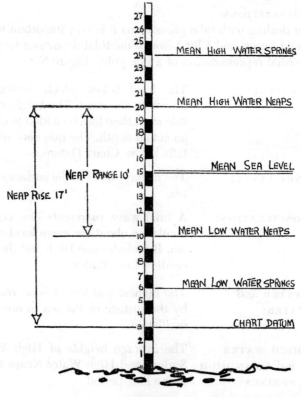

*Figure 8*
*A Tide Pole*

48

near to the Equinoxes, be as much as forty-five feet at Springs, reducing to around sixteen feet at Neaps, but these are quite exceptional for the British Isles where the average range is nearer to the fifteen and twenty foot mark.

The interval of time between one High and the following Low Water around these islands is about six hours fifteen minutes, and High or Low Water will fall on average about fifty minutes later than High Water or Low Water on the previous day. A rough and ready indication of the amount of rise or fall of the tide over a six hour period may be taken as follows:

| | |
|---|---|
| 1st hour: | 1/12th the range |
| 2nd hour: | 2/12ths the range |
| 3rd hour: | 3/12ths the range |
| 4th hour: | 3/12ths the range |
| 5th hour: | 2/12ths the range |
| 6th hour: | 1/12th the range |

TIDAL INFORMATION

The times of both High and Low Water with their corresponding heights are published in tide tables annually. The Admiralty Tide Tables (Vol. 1) covers European Waters and is available from any agent for the sale of Admiralty charts.

Information on the direction and strength of the tidal stream is given on all but the large scale charts in a tabulated form. The tidal stream situation for every hour up to six hours before and after High Water at an adjacent port listed in the Admiralty Tide Tables is given for selected positions on the chart.

For a more all-embracing appreciation of the tidal streams however, the 'Pocket Tidal Stream Atlas' published by the Hydrographer of the Navy for the area in question is well worth obtaining. These cost very little and there are eleven of them, obtainable from any Admiralty Chart Agent: there are clear instructions on how to use them printed on the first page and the areas they embrace are as follows:

The English and Bristol Channels
The Channel Islands and adjacent coasts of France
Approaches to Portland
The Solent and adjacent waters

Dover Strait
Thames Estuary
North Sea (Southern portion)
North Sea (Flamborough Head to Pentland Firth)
Orkney and Shetland Islands
North Coast of Ireland and West Coast of Scotland
Irish Sea

Now that we have a basic knowledge of causes and effects and where to obtain the information as to the height and speed of tide and tidal streams, how is this going to be of use to us?

We have already considered the importance of knowing the height of the tide when entering estuaries with sand bars, and of course it will be necessary to know whether there is sufficient water at any place to proceed with the boat—a fact that any sailor will appreciate who uses tidal waters.

### TIDAL STREAM IN ESTUARIES

An equally important aspect of tides is the behaviour of the flow of water, and we will deal with this in tidal estuaries first.

It is an observed fact that the moment of High Water (which remember in an estuary is synchronised with the turn of the tidal stream) takes place earlier at the mouth of an estuary than at its upper reaches. Incidentally, the times of High Water extracted from the tide tables are calculated for the mouth of such estuaries. What is perhaps not so generally known is that the moment of change of the flow within an estuary will almost always commence earlier within a short distance of the estuary banks than it will at its centre. Frequently with the first turn of the tide one will find the centre deep water still flowing in the original direction while it has already started the contrary flow at the banks: it is worth remembering if trying to get back to one's moorings before the change of tide!

Another fact worth remembering is that the outer edge of a curve in tidal waters—just as with the current in a river—is always scoured deeper and will be faster flowing on both ebb and flood tide than the inner edge of the curve where often there is a deposit of silt, sand and mud because of the slower movement which allows it to settle there.

## TIDAL STREAMS ALONG THE COAST

Except at specific points where some constriction is taking place, such as round headlands and between islands, the strength of the tidal stream along a coast will be very much less than that experienced in an estuary. Nevertheless when the constrictions mentioned above do interfere with the stream, the result is often quite enough to founder a small dayboat.

Take headlands and promontories first: one may argue that there is no constriction evident, since there is the whole expanse to seaward of the obstruction for the water to use, rather than become constricted. This is wrong of course, for it is the fact that there is this expanse of water to seaward which constricts the close inshore water in its flow round a headland: it just cannot get the 'lebensraum' necessary and therefore is squeezed between the headland and the body of the sea farther out. This results in a rapid speeding up of the flow (as does any venturi action of this sort on a flowing medium), and considerable turbulence can result. At Spring Tides particularly, when the flow is strongest halfway between High and Low Water, a small craft should keep well clear of such headlands. If the wind happens to be against the tidal stream a vicious sea can develop in which a small boat might not survive. These phenomena are known as 'races'—they are in fact just that, in so far as the water starts to 'race' round the obstruction. See Figure 9.

If there are rocks lying off the headland or promontory, which is frequently the case since the headland is often a rocky outcrop which carries on beneath the water, these will violently disturb the smooth flow of water deep down on the bottom, causing it to 'boil' up to the surface down tide of the rocks themselves. After the war I spent five years demolishing wrecks, and one of the most valuable methods of the preliminary location of these large obstructions lying on the bottom of an otherwise level seabed was the 'boil' caused by just this disturbance straight down tide from the wreck herself. The distance of the 'boil' from the position of the wreck depended on the depth in which she had sunk, being farther away the deeper the water. At Spring Tides it was quite sufficient to throw a thirty foot power launch around and make her hard to steer. When in addition a sea was running it could make life difficult!

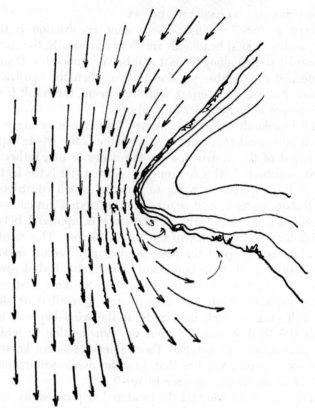

**Figure 9**

*A tidal 'race' round a headland*
*The area in the vicinity of 'A' can be highly dangerous for a small*
*boat, particularly when wind is blowing against the tidal stream.*
*Races are sometimes experienced as much as two or three miles*
*off a headland.*

Such promontories and headlands as we have just been considering form one of the biggest dangers to the small boat man
on a coastal passage. It is inadvisable to attempt a passage close
inshore to the headland because unless one has local knowledge,
to get safely inside the strong effect of the race would be to
approach the shore within a matter of a few feet, and could

easily result in running on the rocks. At the same time to proceed seawards far enough to clear the race may be inadvisable if sailing under the lee of the land in a strong wind. The only safe answer in such conditions is to arrange it so that one rounds the point as near to slack water as possible, when the tidal stream is about to change direction. The race has then subsided, and this should be 'built in' to your calculations when planning the trip. A race is shown sometimes on a chart by a series of small parallel wavy lines.

Another effect of the tidal stream when coasting is the marked 'set' into bays. The stream, on coming to a deep indentation of the coast, will tend to follow the shoreline and this results in a flow as illustrated in Figure 10. Of course, at the other end of the bay one will experience a similar set out again. One should bear this in mind.

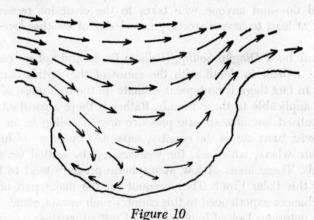

*Figure 10*

*The 'set' of a tidal stream into and out of a bay*

Often, behind a headland one will experience a 'back eddy' as shown in Figure 10 and sometimes this effect is so marked that the water in the whole bay will be swirling in the opposite direction to the main stream out in open water. It can be most useful when fighting an adverse tide, but remember that on reaching the end of the bay you are going to meet an even stronger adverse tide than out in the open water: you can't have your salt biscuits and eat them!

We have already discussed the disturbing effect of contra-blowing winds on the flow of a tidal stream, which make the surface waves shorten up and start breaking, and when this is experienced against a race you may be sure there will be a nasty area of water off the head which you should avoid at all cost. We shall be giving this a deal of thought during the cruise later. Now let us pass on to the causes of that wind; in a nutshell—the weather.

WEATHER LORE

Here in the British Isles we lie slap on the Polar Front which is a broad area running roughly E.N.E.–W.S.W. along which a cold Northerly airstream meets a warm and more moisture laden South Westerly airstream. This is unfortunate so far as stability of climate is concerned but it keeps us very much on our toes—or should do—and anyone who takes to the coast for recreation ought at least to have a working knowledge of weather forecasting.

In my book *Dinghy Sailing* (Pelham Books and Sphere paperbacks) I dealt in detail with the cause of the earth's climatic belts. In fact there is no typical 'climate' in the true sense of that word applicable to these islands. Rather is there a constant flux of localised low atmospheric pressure areas swirling in an anticlockwise twist across the country, separated by ridges of higher pressure where, with luck, the weather can be settled for short periods. These areas of low atmospheric pressure tend to form along this Polar Front. They account for the major part of the disturbances experienced in this country such as rain, wind shifts and a notorious lack of long periods of settled weather.

But there is a certain broadly predictable pattern of events once one knows the situation just to the West of our country. For this information one cannot do better than refer to the daily weather maps published in *The Times* on page two, or to the really excellent satellite photographs of cloud formations over the British Isles which appear in the yachting newspaper *Yachting and Boating Weekly*. This latter paper is available on Wednesdays and prints the satellite photograph for the previous Sunday. When used in conjunction with *The Times* weather maps it gives a more easily visualised picture of what is going on—and what goes on does tend to form a distressingly familiar pattern! When we have looked into the broad principle behind the formation of a typical depression we will analyse one of these weather maps and see how it may help us to arrive at an inspired guess about the weather just due to arrive.

### DEVELOPMENT OF A DEPRESSION (CYCLONE)

In a very simplified form, what happens along the Polar Front is this. The cool North Easterly airstream sweeps diagonally down and meets the warmer South Westerly airstream. This meeting takes place along a broad line bounded roughly by Latitudes 35° and 60° North. Much depends on the time of the year, and the Polar Front tends to shift down to the Southern region within these limits during the winter.

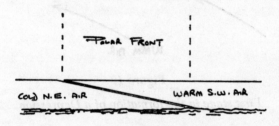

*Figure 11*

*Sectional view of the Polar Front showing the 'scarf joint' effect at junction of the two airstreams.*

Since warm air can hold more water vapour than cold air, and warm air being less dense must rise above cold air by the law of convection, when these two airstreams meet they do not just continue to slide along the face of one another in a vertical wall. Instead the cold air undercuts the warm air so that what may be thought of as a huge 'scarf joint' in air is established right along the Polar Front. In section it would like Figure 11.

Once this situation is established, the line of the Polar Front running E.N.E.–W.S.W. does not remain straight. Sooner or later a wave, or undulation, begins to form in a horizontal plane. This is the birth place of a depression or area of low atmospheric pressure—often called a 'low' for short. This wave formation results in a bulge of warm air encroaching up into the Northern area of the Polar Front. By the same action the two adjacent bulges of cold (and less moisture laden) air encroach down into the warmer Southern area of the Front. In plan the Polar Front now looks like Figure 12.

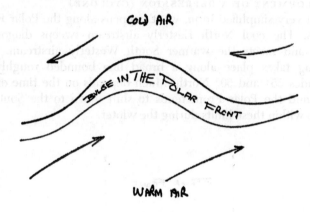

*Figure 12*

*First stage in the formation of a Depression.*

It does not stop there, however. The tip of the bulge continues probing Northward and a wedge of warm air is soon formed trapped between the cold air at either side. But warm air which is surrounded more or less by cold air must rise and in doing so forms an area of reduced pressure beneath it, into which the cold air has to flow. Air in a high pressure area will always flow in to fill a low pressure area.

As soon as this 'sucking in' action on the cold surrounding air really gets moving in terms of actual motion of large air masses, a vast inward spiralling whirlpool results which, in meteorological language is called 'cyclonic'. This whirlpool effect is quite logical and is due to the rotation of the earth on its axis and is always in an anti-clockwise direction in the Northern hemisphere.

The whole developing cyclonic system is, in addition to its own rotation, probably moving at anything between five and sixty sea miles per hour E.N.E. up the line of the Polar Front. It tends to move along the Polar Front faster in the early stages of formation, slowing down as it becomes more developed. If the original bulge formed out in the Atlantic, the developing depression will, nine times out of ten, be heading our way.

Within the cyclone this is what takes place: the Western side of the wedge, where the cold air is undercutting the warm air at ground level, sweeps down and round anti-clockwise, butting the warm air quite violently up above it in a fairly sharp incline. This side of the wedge is called the cold front. The Eastern side of the wedge tends similarly to be swirling anti-clockwise, but due to the fact that the cold air is being pushed in a direction contrary to its original flow from the North East, and also because it is dragging back from a surface area of earth with which it had already been in contact, friction tends to slow down the advance and elongate the 'scarf joint' effect on this front. This Eastern edge is called the warm front. The warm air flows over the top of the cold air in a shallow incline and the whole front tends to swirl round more slowly than the advancing cold front behind it.

The result is an ever narrowing wedge of warm air, with low pressure developing at its apex and the whole wedge gradually closing up rather like a curved scissor blade with the hinge at the apex of the wedge. Up there at the apex, where the warm air has lost contact with the ground and is now cushioned on cold air, an 'occlusion' is said to have taken place. It will look something like Figure 13.

## THE EFFECT OF A DEPRESSION

In idealised form we now have a well developed 'low', or depression. What can it mean to you and me in terms of wind and visibility?

Here we must consider the units of measurement and the symbols which meteorologists use in order that we can begin to speak in other than purely relative terms.

Pressure of our atmosphere is measured in units called millibars. One millibar is equal to a pressure of one thousand dynes per square centimetre. Don't worry about that: the point is that at the centre of a well developed 'low' the pressure can be around 965 millibars, while in an area of high pressure it can be around 1040 millibars. So you see the full range of pressure extremes we experience is somewhere around 75 millibars, and this will give a relative framework which is of use. The aneroid barometer is the instrument used to measure these pressures and is generally calibrated in millibars, although some of the older ones are still calibrated in inches. 970 millibars is just over 28½ inches, while 1040 millibars is just over 30½ inches, so you will appreciate that the millibar scale allows of greater accuracy.

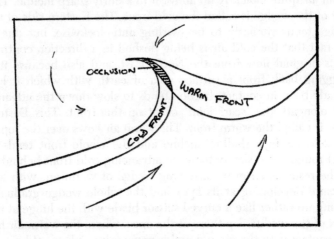

*Figure 13*

*An established depression, occluded at its apex. Arrows indicate the spiralling-in of airstreams.*

The warm front on a weather map is marked with black half circles on its advancing edge, while the cold front is marked with black triangles on its advancing edge. Where an occlusion has taken place alternate black half circles and triangles are put on the line.

Areas of equal pressure are joined by thin lines called isobars, and against these lines the pressure is printed in millibars rather like a contour map but the pressure in millibars takes the place of the height in feet.

Now let us look at the situation we have developed above in terms of a weather map, using the correct symbols. Figure 14 shows our depression with the occlusion, cold front, warm front and isobars superimposed upon it. We have to remember that the wind is circulating anti-clockwise around that centre of 970 millibars and spiralling inward as it does so, to form a slight angle with the lines of the isobars.

You will notice I have drawn a line A–B just South of the centre of the depression, and I want you to imagine you are standing with a barometer, thermometer, and compass at ground level directly in the path of this depression at point A. As it passes overhead, you will appear to be moving down the line A–B.

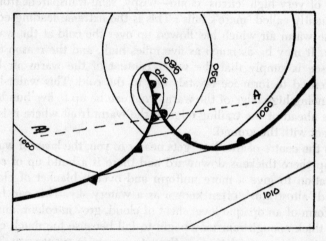

*Figure 14*

*How a depression is shown on the weather map.*

We will observe what you might well experience in terms of wind shifts and force, visibility, changes of pressure and changes of temperature as it does so.

At point A, prior to the arrival of the situation shown, the wind could well have been from a South Westerly direction, but as the depression approaches this will probably 'back' to a more Southerly point. This is because that 'spiralling-in' effect is beginning to be felt. Notice here that the term 'back' when speaking of the wind means that it is changing direction with an anti-clockwise motion. If it swings with a clockwise motion it is said to be 'veering'.

The sky at point A—before the effect of the advancing 'low' was beginning to be felt—was probably typical of a South Westerly airstream; overcast with occasional hill fog or drizzle in winter, or humid with hazy sunshine in summer. Or, if the wind happened to have been settled from the North West, it might well have been clear with the odd cumuliform cloud (cotton wool type) giving occasional showers. The barometer would be reading around 1000 millibars with a slight tendency to fall.

The first visual sign of the approaching 'low' often takes the form of very high 'cirrus' cloud—wispy, semi-transparent fronds frequently called 'mare's tails'. This is the extreme leading edge of the warm air which has flowed up over the cold at the warm front. It may be as much as five miles high, and the reason one can see is simply that the water content of the warm air has condensed to form ice crystals due to the cold. This wafer-like advancing high edge of the warm front can be up to five hundred miles ahead of the trailing edge of the warm front where it is in contact with the ground.

As the centre of the 'low' gets nearer to you, the layer of warm air up there thickens downward and there is a build up of condensation to give a more uniform and overall blanket of cloud called 'altostratus', often known as a watery sky. This can take the form of an opaque level sheet of cloud, grey in colour, and if it is thick enough rain may begin to fall because too much condensation is accumulating up there to remain in suspension. The warm front at ground level may now be some two hundred miles to the West. The barometer will be falling steadily, and if there is a wind shift it will tend to continue backing toward the South and increase in force. If the barometer starts falling at a rate of one millibar per hour or more you can expect some strong winds because it will mean that the isobars are close together—closer than on our weather map—and this means there is going to be a quick change of pressure which is conducive to violent wind responses. The temperature now may start to rise a little since there is a good deal of mixing taking place between the two airstreams.

As the wedge thickens yet more, 'nimbo-stratus' cloud will form—thick and dark grey. Its lower edge may possibly be broken off and whipped about by the increasing wind force into 'scud', which is the name given to low lying ragged detached bits of these clouds: fairly ominous looking. The barometer will continue to fall. On our weather map it will be reading about 985 millibars and the rate at which it is falling is a sure indication of the severity of the depression. Rain may be continuous now.

With the actual passage over you of the warm front at ground level, the temperature will rise, the wind probably veer to about S.W. or W.S.W. and in our example the barometer will sit steady at around 975 millibars. The rain may ease or cease altogether but there may be a noticeable 'mugginess' or humidity in the air, since you are now in the heart of the warm moisture laden air section.

Next comes the cold front and here, since it is steeper in its inclination than the retreating warm front, the changes in cloud form, temperature, and pressure will be more rapid. This results in more violent responses from the wind.

Remember the actual apex of the wedge (the centre of the depression) is up there North of you in our example. You may visualise how as it moves across toward the North East the inward spiralling wind which is affecting you in the warm sector will tend to veer quite rapidly to the North West when the cold front arrives. It will almost certainly freshen as it does so. The warm air now starts climbing again rapidly above you, forming violent 'cumulus' clouds which can bring thunderstorms. The barometer starts rising again and the temperature tends to drop. These cumulus clouds are large rolling cotton wool formations which look altogether too solid to stay up there. They have white tops and grey undersides where the sunlight cannot shine on them and there is generally brilliant clear blue sky in between them. They bring squally rain showers and a treacherous gusty wind.

As the trailing edge of the cold front passes away there may be 'cumulo nimbus' cloud formation high up. This is cumulus cloud with flattened tops which trail away from the main body. The flattened areas are almost certainly formed of ice crystals, and again therefore we may see the wispy cirrus, or mare's tails up there which signify the last of the depression just as they indicated the beginning of it. The barometer during this period will have risen to stabilise again somewhere around 990 or 1000 millibars and the temperature will have fallen yet more. If the wind stays in the North West we can expect clear skies and the odd cumulus clouds giving occasional showers.

Such is the probable pattern of a very straightforward and simplified depression the centre of which passes North of an observer. Figure 15 gives a visual impression of the sequence of events very much compressed and not at all to scale but it will help you to understand the overall picture.

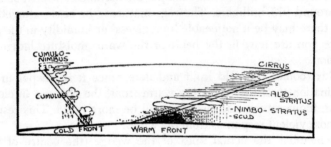

*Figure 15*

*Cross section of a depression.*
*The dark area shows heavy rain.*

From the foregoing you will understand the logic in the old saying that if you stand with your back to the wind, the centre of the depression (in the Northern hemisphere) will lie to your left-hand side. It must be so, since the wind is swirling around the centre in an inward spiralling anti-clockwise direction. South of the equator it circles the other way round!

But these depressions are seldom as uncomplicated as this example. Secondary depressions can form on the advancing fronts which may develop fast while the original main depression occludes and fills up. Or the whole depression may occlude before it reaches you in which case no actual passage of warm and cold fronts will be experienced as such by an observer on the ground. Even so, from an understanding of this oversimplified example you will have a good foundation for making a workmanlike assessment of what is arriving, provided you have the basic information of what lies just to the West in the form of a weather map.

It is worth mentioning however that on occasions, in between these Polar Front 'lows', a highly localised non-frontal 'low' can form in an unstable airstream (showery weather). These small but sometimes quite violent depressions are known as Polar Lows and are often too small to be detected by weather-plotting stations which are fairly widely separated. But their effect on a sailor can be just as violent as any other depression—and often more unexpected!

So much for cyclones.

ANTICYCLONES OR 'HIGHS'

What of their opposites, the anticyclones, which are the established centres of high pressure and generally associated with more or less good weather and steady winds?

In an anticyclone the wind spirals outwards from the high pressure centre towards the low pressure surrounds, circulating in a clockwise direction in the Northern hemisphere. Since the air near the centre is inclined to be denser and heavier than its surrounding air and therefore tends to subside, it is this which, by inhibiting any convectional effect, does make for a more stable system than the cyclones. These anticyclones frequently form just South and to the West of the British Isles and have an annoying habit of sticking around the area of the Azores instead of working their way North Eastward to Britain. In fact, once developed they tend to move very little.

On looking at a weather map, if we find ourselves on the edge of a 'high', whatever winds we may be experiencing at the time will tend to remain steady and of moderate strength. If there is a marked haze at ground level you may assume that the 'high' is fairly well established and can be expected to stay for a while because these anticyclones are vast, very slow moving masses of air. If the 'high' is sitting right on top of the observer the weather pattern will remain stable, but the winds are likely to be much lighter and variable in direction. This is because local convectional disturbances (such as a sea breeze on to a shoreline in the daytime) are able to superimpose themselves on the overall pattern—which they cannot do nearer the perimeter due to the stronger anticyclonic wind.

A sea breeze is caused when the land heats up faster than the sea during the day. The air over the warmer land will rise, thus pulling the colder air from over the sea in beneath it. This breeze will die as the land cools down towards evening.

It is in just these circumstances that a dinghy sailor on observing a sea breeze develop may set off out from the mouth of an estuary—probably on the top of High Water—intending nothing more than an hour or so's jaunt. However, this sea breeze will almost certainly die away, leaving him with a hard row back probably against the adverse tidal stream!

On days when a 'high' is established over this country it often pays the dinghy sailor to launch early and proceed seawards to pick up this developing onshore breeze as the land gets warmer during the late morning. Sometimes these sea breezes can become moderate to fresh in strength, easing as the day becomes older. This easing is the sign for him to get back shorewards as soon as possible otherwise he may need the 'wooden topsails'—oars.

These sea breezes can, when blowing on to a shoreline, establish the wind pattern of a localised 'high'. Take for example a situation where the centre of a large 'high' is to the North of the shoreline over the sea: the wind will already have a tendency to be blowing from the North East, and as the sea breeze effect is felt, it may set up its own tendency to swirl clockwise, veering during the day along the coastline and thus augmenting the overall wind pattern. If the prevailing wind were off shore however due to the 'high' being to the South over the land, the South Westerly wind caused by a 'high' in this position will tend to be diminished by the sea breeze.

COASTAL FOG

Coastal sailors will do well to remember that if the sea should be relatively warmer than the land the air above the water will be carrying more moisture which will form fog on arrival at the coast due to its cooling on reaching the land. This can obliterate navigational objects just inland such as churches and the like.

Another cause of highly localised fog in estuaries around our coastline is the fact that river water in the estuary is often cooler than the sea into which it flows. If a warm moisture laden airstream is coming in off the sea it may then form thick fog over the estuary due to immediate condensation.

1. *Sand bar at mouth of Camel Estuary.*

Above: *Low water Spring tide. Bar is shown with waves breaking across whole width of mouth.* Below: *Half tide, flood (eight feet more depth). All activity appeared to have ceased when the breaker shown materialised.*

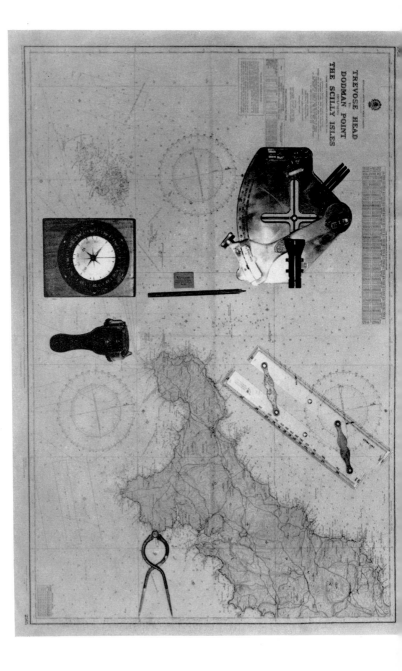

2. *Navigation: the tools for the job. Chart, steering compass, hand-bearing compass, parallel ruler, dividers, sextant, pencil and soft rubber.*

## SEA FOG

By the same effect, when warm moisture laden air flows from above relatively warm water across colder water it will condense to form thick fog. The well known example of this is the moist South Westerly wind coming into contact with the cold Labrador current off the Grand Banks, but it can happen more locally in our coastal waters.

Reverting to our anticyclone for a moment, if this is declining —by that I mean not moving away but simply dispersing—it will almost certainly show the fact by a disappearance of the haze at ground level while the wind remains light, and it can happen very gradually over two or three days. But one which has started to move away will more likely show the fact by a retention of the haziness but an increase in the wind strength.

## WEATHER INFORMATION

Used in conjunction with the radio Land and Shipping forecasts, the weather maps can make a lot of sense, and in this respect the services of the Meteorological office via the B.B.C. are really first class. The shipping forecasts are essentially for sailors who are concerned more with wind speeds, direction and visibility. The land weather forecast is aimed at the holiday-maker or farmer who is perhaps more concerned with the temperature, sunshine or rain and they do often omit any reference to wind direction and speed which can be infuriating to a sailor! But they are often of use to the dayboat sailor because they do sometimes mention specifically the coastal wind such as a sea breeze. Full details of times of forecasts are given in the *Radio Times* and there is an excellent pull-out supplement in *Reeds Nautical Almanac* which gives this information.

Figure 16 shows a map of the British Isles with the shipping forecast areas superimposed. These forecasts give the wind strength in terms of the Beaufort Scale, and this is detailed in Figure 17.

To summarise then, before taking to the water, you should get your weather forecast and be aware of the general weather state indicated by the weather maps, either from the newspapers or television so that you not only know the immediate forecast but what is in the vicinity. This should then be related to the result-

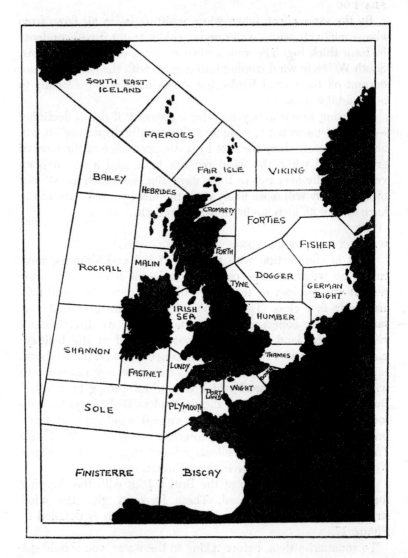

*Figure 16*
*Shipping Forecast Areas*

ing sea conditions you are likely to meet. A knowledge of weather lore will also help you to interpret quickly any noticeable deviation from the forecast weather pattern.

This has been of necessity a short summary and any sailor would find it rewarding to study the many specialised books on the subject.

| Wind force | Speed in knots | Wind description, and reaction of a small craft handler. |
|---|---|---|
| 0 | Less than one knot | No wind. Splendid for powerboats. |
| 1 | 1–3 | Light airs. Drifting match for dinghies. Powerboat operators still very happy. |
| 2 | 4–6 | Light breeze. Dinghies now hopeful. Powerboat operators happy. |
| 3 | 7–10 | Gentle breeze. Dinghies come to life. Powerboat operators don oilskins. |
| 4 | 11–16 | Moderate breeze. Dinghy sailing exciting. Powerboat operators begin to seek a lee. |
| 5 | 17–21 | Fresh breeze. Inexperienced dinghy sailors wisely discover defects in their boats. Experienced dinghy sailors become enthusiastic and cause defects in their boats. Powerboat operators reduce speed. |
| 6 | 22–27 | A strong breeze. All dinghy sailors but the madheads go home. Powerboat operators, at reduced speed, start eyeing the size of waves. |
| 7 | 28–33 | Near gale. All but fools stay ashore. |
| 8 | 34–40 | Gale. Those with sense take their boats out of the water and tie securely down. |
| 9 | 41–47 | Strong gale. Scrutinize insurance policies. |
| 10 | 48–55 | Storm. We read about it in the papers for days afterwards. Better get the boat off the beach or hard. |
| 11 | 56–63 | Violent storm. Is she under cover in a boatyard? |
| 12 | Above 63 | Hurricane. Where is the boatyard? |

Remember that the shipping forecasts give wind details for the open sea and this will be influenced by the type of land in close proximity to your cruising water.

The telephone number of your local Met. Office is given at the front of the telephone directory under the heading 'Facilities and Services'.

*Figure 17*

*Beaufort wind scale*

# 3

# The Expertise of
# Boat Handling

A great part of seamanship lies in knowing the capabilities of one's boat, and as stated at the opening of Chapter One, a skipper, in addition to being sure of his own abilities, should also be aware of the way his craft will react in different situations.

### THE SHAPE OF IT

It will pay us first to look at some slightly larger craft which are meant to operate in the open sea, for we can learn much from their lines which can equally be applied to the small dayboat.

Look at a deep-sea fishing trawler. Here is a small ship which has to 'keep the sea' and survive the worst it can throw at her. You will see a bow which has a marked 'flare'—turning outward at the top so as to provide more and more buoyancy the deeper it is immersed. The line of the hull then flows down to a minimum freeboard about two-thirds of the way back, rising again to give good freeboard aft. You will notice too that the stern more often than not slopes in toward the waterline as illustrated in Figure 18. This shape has not been evolved from any consideration of comfort, but solely from the necessity to ride out any state of sea, and from the foregoing survey of sea conditions you may understand why such a shape does just this.

A power craft so shaped at the bow will be able to ease her way gently into the wind and against all but the largest of freak waves without burying her bow and becoming swamped. The flare, as well as giving added buoyancy, will tend to throw the water back from her bow so that no heavy quantity of water comes aboard. The low middle section of the boat, sometimes almost excessively low in these trawlers, is there so that the men may easily work their fishing gear. These craft often have long sea trips to their fishing grounds, and while getting out there or returning with their catch, as well as steaming into the seas they are likely to have to run long distances before the seas, steaming that is in the same direction as the waves. While the stern will not have to punch its way into the waves it will nevertheless have to

*Figure 18*

*The hull lines of a typical deep-sea trawler*

ride them out as they overtake the ship. This is why she is shaped aft to give a good degree of lift by sloping under toward the waterline. It is called a 'counter' stern.

Don't think however that when running in this fashion the bow becomes redundant. As the stern lifts to a large following wave so the bow drops down into the trough ahead of the wave and here again the large buoyancy reserve forward is essential. Many small boats have been driven under by a large following wave lifting the stern to the point where the buoyancy at the bow was overcome, thus allowing the craft to dip her foredeck under the surface. You will appreciate that this happens when the vessel is accelerating down the forward slope of a wave, and once the bow buries there is a tremendous resistance right forward and low down, to any more forward movement. In extreme cases this can result in the stern somersaulting more or less right over the bow. 'Pitchpoling' is the term used to describe this frightful event and it has happened to me in a small boat just once on a bar at the mouth of an estuary.

Miles Smeeton in his book *Once is Enough* gives a graphic description of how his forty-six foot ketch, 'Tzu Hang', was pitchpoled nine hundred miles off Cape Horn. Those were quite exceptional seas and 'Tzu Hang's crew were quite exceptional sailors or they would not have survived to tell us about it.

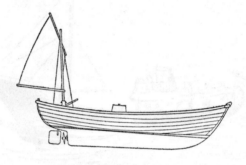

*Figure 19*

*The 18½ foot Dell Quay 'Fisherboat'*

Neither you nor I are likely to acquire or want a deep-sea trawler but we can learn from their lines, for there is much about them which is equally applicable to a small open powerboat when assessing her ability to ride out a sea.

The well known 18½ foot Dell Quay 'Fisherboat' is a good example of a small seaworthy open power launch. See Figure 19. In the major respects she follows the same shape—the rise and flare at the bow, with a smaller rise to the stern—but in this case she has what is often called a Norwegian stern. She comes to a point at both bow and stern, but the stern has no flare. These 'double enders' are good seaboats. Being small they do not of course have as much freeboard as their larger sisters, nor do they travel so fast, so it is important that as well as having adequate lift aft, the stern parts the whitecaps as they overtake her, rather like a bow action. Many of the larger motor fishing vessels are similarly shaped—and they are also acknowledged as being among the most seaworthy of powered craft. Note also the Fisherboat's mizzen sail for dampening down the rolling, and keeping her head-to-wind and sea when required.

Another perfect example of 'double enders', of course, are the Royal National Lifeboats. They have to punch into and run before the worst of seas at speeds around eight to ten knots. Plate 3 shows a 'Solent' class lifeboat undergoing righting tests. It gives an idea of her underwater lines and the tremendous buoyancy and inherent stability: that crane hoist is still pulling her over though she is already some 125 degrees off the vertical!

While on the subject of powered craft I would like here to draw your attention to a completely different type of hull—that of a high speed powerboat. Make no mistake, some of these are excellent seaboats but not in the sense that we have just been considering. The essential difference is that when the sea gets angry a low speed craft (either power or sail) survives by giving the sea its head. The only way she CAN survive is to diminish as much as possible the power of the water and wind by defensive action such as 'heaving to', laying out a sea anchor or warps, or just reducing sail or power thus reducing speed to ease conditions.

The high speed powerboat—I'm talking now of the craft that punch along in the region of thirty knots or more—take the sea by storm and are not primarily intended or designed to put to sea in really rough conditions. They are the aggressors and they crash along sometimes literally leaping from wave to wave which brings tremendous stresses to bear on their hulls. See Plate 4. Entirely different considerations govern design, primarily the strength to withstand the enormous thrust from their engines and the resultant hammer blows from the sea on the underparts, linked with large reserves of stability. This stability is not only from a gravitational point of view such as 'weight down low', which is predominantly the case in craft designed to flow slowly through the water. But in addition this fast powerboat design has to take into consideration the distribution of shock pressure on the under surfaces of the hull. When two or three tons of hull travelling at forty knots crashes down on to the next wave crest

71

ahead (having gone completely over the trough!) it is vital that the upward resistance of water acts as evenly as possible over a fairly large area of hull bottom. If the hull were shaped so that this enormous pressure could concentrate perhaps at one point only of the flattish sharply angled bottom she could twist right over.

This is what takes such tremendous skill and fitness when handling these racing powerboats: it is imperative that you catch that wave ahead at just the right angle! Crews have been known to break their legs simply by being caught with straight knees when they should have been slightly bent to absorb the shock as the hull slams down. Handling this type of craft calls for a high degree of seamanship, but of a very specialised form quite different to the sort we shall be thinking about in the pages which follow.

The shape of a sailing craft, large or small, has to cater for one additional factor which does not concern the powerboat. To convert power from the wind into forward propulsion the underparts of the hull must resist sideways pressure, and in order to prevent the resultant heeling due to the point at which this pressure is exerted—on the sails—she has to have either a heavy weight down low beneath the hull itself, or a large amount of buoyancy well away from the centreline which results in what is called 'straddle stability' or, in the really small craft, a shifting weight which can be slung quickly out over the weather side— the crew.

Look at the lines of the T.24 in Figure 20. This is a good example of the medium-sized offshore sailing cruiser/racer, and you will immediately see that her ballasted keel (1.2 tons) is right down where it will be exerting a gravitational righting influence immediately she heels, and the more she heels the more she will try to come upright. The hull shape on the other hand is very different from the powerboat line. Here there can be no low middle section, for if there were when the boat was heeling hard she would have her deck amidships permanently under. They do, on occasions, but it is not from choice and adds considerably to the resistance to forward motion.

The underwater shape, in addition to having to accommodate that heavy keel down below it also has to offer strong lateral

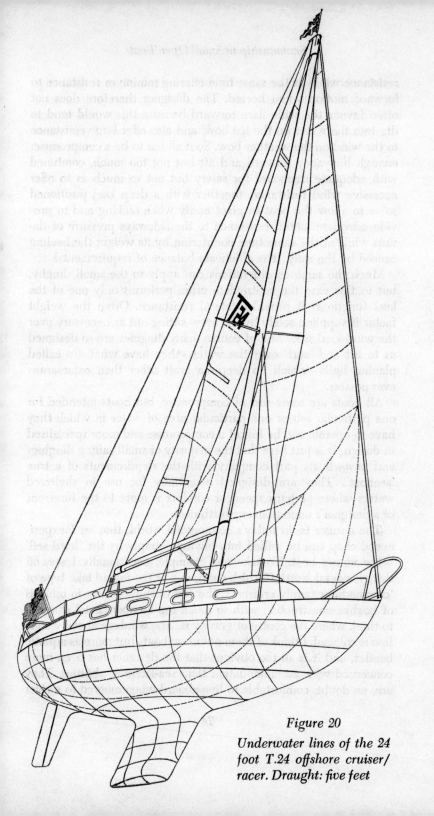

Figure 20

*Underwater lines of the 24 foot T.24 offshore cruiser/ racer. Draught: five feet*

resistance while at the same time offering minimum resistance to forward motion when heeled. The designer therefore does not often favour the wide flare forward because this would tend to dig into the water on the lee bow, and also offer large resistance to the wind on the weather bow. So it all has to be a compromise: enough buoyancy forward and aft but not too much, combined with adequate freeboard for safety but not so much as to offer excessive wind resistance, together with a deep keel positioned so as to allow the boat to pivot easily when tacking and to provide adequate lateral resistance to the sideways pressure of the sails while at the same time countering by its weight the heeling caused by the sails. It is a delicate balance of requirements!

Much the same considerations can apply to the small dinghy, but in this case the centreplate often performs only one of the keel functions: it provides lateral resistance. Often the weight factor is supplied solely by the crew sitting out as necessary over the windward side. And of course many dinghies are so designed as to lift and 'surf' over the water—they have what are called planing hulls—which no deep-sea craft other than catamarans ever possess.

All boats are some sort of compromise, but boats intended for one particular job or one particular area of water in which they have to operate can be less of a compromise and more specialised in design. It is just here that the majority of small sailing dinghies and powerboats part company with the requirements of a true 'seaboat'. They are designed essentially for use in sheltered waters where perhaps speed or comfort is more to the forefront of a designer's mind than seaworthiness.

The danger is, in today's commercial world, that an inexperienced chap can be gulled into buying—simply by the 'hard sell' —the wrong boat. To take one example, occasionally I see, off this elemental North Cornish coast, one of the inland lake type of 'commodious family cruisers'. The sort of thing I have in mind is of boxlike construction with so much top-hamper that I shudder to think where the centre of gravity is. The windage above waterline is colossal. I think of them not as seaboats but more as aquatic beetles, and it is all too obvious that the designer has been more concerned with accommodation than sea-keeping abilities. They are, no doubt, comfortable to live aboard when moored to a river bank, but ought never to proceed farther to seaward than the harbour master's cat.

Bear in mind that the more specialised a design becomes, the less capable it is of operating in conditions different from those for which it is intended.

HAPPY TURTLE.

— NO FARTHER SEEAWARD THAN THE HARBOURMASTER'S CAT !

It is not the object of this book to teach the basic theory of handling small powerboats or sailing dinghies. Throughout I have assumed that the reader is already competent to sail a dinghy or drive a speedboat or power launch from one point to another.

What I do propose doing is to consider those awkward situations which arise, calling for considerable expertise beyond the normal handling ability. We will deal with them in two groups, power and sail.

### BOAT HANDLING UNDER POWER

Remember we are thinking here of small open dayboats in the ten to eighteen foot range. These fall into two main groups, speedboats and launches. Speedboats today are more often than not propelled by outboard motors or perhaps by stern-drive 'Z' units in which a powerful engine is sited just inboard of the transom, both such types being steered by altering the angle of thrust of the propeller. Launches generally have a lower powered much slower revving inboard engine, a propeller which is capable of thrusting in two directions only, forward or reverse, and are steered with a rudder generally abaft the propeller. There is a world of difference in their handling characteristics.

Take the speedboats first. If I may range broadly across this form of water sport, I would like to point out that two things should be constantly borne in mind by every driver. First, the majority of dinghy sailors within aural and visual range will consider you a menace. They may not voice this opinion—certainly not in the club bar if they're psychologists—but deep in the confessional of their hearts, most of them think it. Second, bear in mind that you are a menace. You are a menace because they think you are, and the irony of it is that very often it's nothing whatever to do with you! It has to do with nervousness. Indeed, my neck is fairly flexible, so I'll make a further true statement. Competence afloat, as in most fields of human activity, is almost always in inverse proportion to nervousness. A person who feels he can handle a situation more often than not actually can handle it. A person who is doubtful about it generally makes a mess of things.

Back to speedboats: just visualise the situation . . . there you go with your plume of spray, serenely happy, serenely competent, sizing up the situations as they develop . . . the dinghy over there that's just tacking, this chap over here in goggles and flippers, his backside in the air, his eyes on the bottom . . . the ferry just casting off from the jetty: plenty of room everywhere, who's worrying?

See it through the eyes of that chap in the ten foot 'hopeful' class sailing dinghy, almost becalmed, probably with the tiller hard over trying to change tacks but making sternway; '. . . has this chap in the speedboat seen me? He's coming right AT me! (You're three hundred yards away.) Can't he SEE I'm here! Why can't I get this damned thing about! What DO I DO . . . I CAN'T get out of HIS way!' And so it goes on. Tow a couple of water-skiers behind you and you will probably see him begin to emulate a duck in a thunderstorm. It's born of nervousness. Sometimes not without cause: he probably saw someone chopped in half by something like you!

Or take that stealthy light-air group of sailing butterflies working the back eddy of tide with main, genoa, spinnaker and the girl friend's blouse catching every ghost of a breath, gaining . . . losing . . . that foot or two of hard earned, concentrated advantage that is just going to make the difference between a silver jug on the mantelpiece or a photo of mother-in-law.

There you go, a hundred yards to leeward and you can't be in the way of any single one of them. How the devil CAN you? Two minutes later the leading boat's spinnaker collapses, the main of the second boat crashes across and the colours are running in the girl friend's blouse . . . a ripple of catastrophic doom fans back through the racing fleet. But you are five hundred yards up the estuary, oblivious, serenely happy with hot ears. No; make no mistake, they don't love you.

I only mention this because it really is up to you, as a driver of a speedboat, to do everything in your power to minimise this 'menace phobia' of the other chap. Your potential 'circle of interference' with other water users is often much larger than you think. Of course, it does not only apply to the other boat either; your own crew or passengers are more or less at your mercy. It may be their idiocy that brings them to harm, but it is your responsibility to see that such idiocy does not take place in your boat. The sort of thing I have in mind is the fast powerboat snaking across the calm water with the delightful bikini-clad figurehead balanced on the stem with feet down either side cooling her toes in the top of the spray. What happens if that engine cuts, or the driver throttles back suddenly? In she goes—straight over the bow, and back under the boat before you can gasp, to be sliced in the propeller. It happens. NEVER allow any member of your crew to go forward of the windscreen when at speed. Keep them back in the cockpit and preferably seated.

Cultivate a habit, when about to surge away from a stationary position in one of these fast powerboats, of saying loudly and clearly, 'We're off!' Then pause, doing nothing. Follow it by the words, 'O.K.?' and *look round at your crew to see that they are*

*either seated or have a firm grip on something secure.* The likelihood is that you will find Lulubelle perched on the after coaming
in the act of adjusting a bathing hat over her cloth ears. You
would have gone . . . but she wouldn't have been with you! And
the nasty part is that propeller.

If turning quickly at speed, or altering course violently—
neither of which you should do without proper warning to your
crew except perhaps in an emergency—there is a very real chance
that one of your crew members can be caught off balance and
fall either forward, backward or sideways. Inertia plays a great
part in these nippy aquatic hot-rods. I have seen one of them
doing somewhere around thirty knots spin right over in a tight
turn due entirely to bad handling. Sea conditions were choppy—
too choppy for the speed the craft was doing, and the wheel was
put hard over just as the hull itself left the water on a wavecrest.
The propeller, giving the boat a violent shove from low down in
a direction angled to the keel, spun the fore-and-aft line across
the line of travel and tilted the hull into the turn. She hit the
water almost broadside on by which time the driver had violently
spun the wheel amidships again. She rolled over twice with the
engine roaring, and the crew of two were thrown out like corks—
luckily clear of the propeller—the boat sank.

Anyone who has changed to a propeller-steered powerboat
after handling a conventional rudder-steered launch will feel
completely at sea until he just remembers that he has no rudder,
and when power is off, the wheel is virtually useless for steering.
Put it hard over and with luck the bow may just begin to look
like swinging after a few seconds provided you have a fair
amount of way on. This is simply because the drive unit is angling
round and presenting rather more resistance to the flow of water
to one side of the keel than the other. But there is no positive
action. That only comes into play when you put her in gear again
—and then it's so alarming in its positive action that until you get
used to thinking 'propeller thrust' all the time, you will probably
begin to wonder if you ever knew anything about boat handling.

With single or twin units, when you put the wheel over and
engage power, a stationary craft will swing on her own axis at
first with hardly any forward movement at all. It's disconcerting;
particularly so when coming alongside a jetty or another craft.

You bring her in perhaps at just too great an angle, and give that slight kick ahead with the wheel over to swing the bow out. Then you decide you're a fraction too fast, so unthinking you give her a kick astern with the throttle. What happens? The propeller was angled so as to kick the stern in towards the jetty when going ahead. Going astern it does just the opposite and sucks the stern violently away from the jetty, crashing the bow into it. With a rudder-steered launch of course virtually no 'slewing' effect would begin to come into play until the craft had stopped moving forward. Only as she gathered sternway would the rudder gradually begin to take effect.

Remember too, when handling these twin unit propeller-steered craft that you are bringing considerable power into play—with no effort other than a slight hand movement of two small levers. Try to imagine the thrust necessary to effect the responses you are causing. If you like, imagine your two hands gripping the bottom of those drive units and pushing, pulling or twisting the hull to obtain the results you do, for it all originates down at the bottom of that drive shaft below the hull. You will wonder how the transom mountings and the machinery itself stand the strain. Of course, in a well-designed boat it is all built so that the greatest possible stresses—thrust, pull or twist—are catered for, but in the hands of an unfeeling operator a boat can, nevertheless, be unfairly punished. She won't last long.

One important word of advice here: in these fast powerboats one very easily becomes fooled into an altogether false 'speed and damage' relationship. The damage sustained by a boat's hull is in exact relationship to the weight of the boat and the speed she is moving. Our friend inertia again. When you have spent the last hour or two careering about at twenty or thirty knots, six or seven knots is relatively almost stopped. So it seems to you. But it is a whacking great crash when you miscalculate and nudge the corner of a jetty at six knots, believe me. Try always to adjust your assessment of speed to a true value by throttling back well in advance of the moment of coming alongside and then treating the boat as you would think of a rowing-boat. It will save you a lot of paint and repair bills.

Now: a few situations. You will of course always choose to make your approach alongside or up to another stationary object so that you are stemming the run of the tide. This is obvious, for you have better control of a boat—no matter what type—when moving through the water. If you can be making way through the water and yet still be stationary in relation to another object you may wish to close—that is ideal, for you can 'hover' at any position you choose in relation to that object.

## GOING TO THE RESCUE UNDER POWER

There she is: a sailing dinghy on her side with two crew members completely exhausted after getting her up four times, only to watch her capsize again. One of them has got the mainsail down and mainsheet and halyards are now, you may assume, wrapped round everything they can come into contact with—shrouds, boom, mast—you name it. The water is choppy and there is a brisk wind. It is the first time you have ever found yourself in a situation where you are called upon to effect a 'rescue'. Bear in mind that a tidal stream so far as your relative movement to the other boat and her crew are concerned will not affect either. You are both floating in the same water, unless either of you becomes in some way attached to the bottom. How are you going to set about it? Your first concern is with the safety of the chaps in the water. Look at them as you approach: have they got buoyancy aids? If not, are they apparently unharmed, and merely wet through and dejected, or is one of them perhaps in a worse state and beginning to look frightened, or even panic stricken?

Decide that first, because on it depends your consequent action. Let us assume that the latter is in fact the case and one of the crew, with no buoyancy aid or lifejacket, is separated from the boat and in danger of drowning. Give him your full attention: the other chap is clinging to the boat and in no immediate danger.

As you approach get your crew, if you have one, to secure your lifebuoy or a spare lifejacket (though the former is better because it is more easily thrown and carries way through the air farther) to a convenient length of line if it has not already one attached (which it should have). The man in the water will be to windward of the capsized boat because that boat is being blown down wind, while the chap in the water is not. You, too, will blow down wind as soon as you have lost any way imparted by your engine. The sea, remember, is choppy. What you must do is to position your powerboat as near to the chap in the water as possible and across the wind from him without actually striking him because there is a lot of movement taking place relative to his head and your hull—in all directions, and particularly up and down.

Think 'propellor' as you get very close, and do nothing which can possibly bring the man and the propeller in contact with each other. Throw the lifebuoy to him and haul him alongside with a helping hand to get him into the boat. The easiest place to do this is over the stern, but that is right into the propeller so disengage the propeller as soon as you see he has a firm hold on the lifebuoy, or cut the engine completely if you have no gear.

If it should be that the victim is already beyond helping himself, even to the extent of holding on to the lifebuoy while being hauled to the boat, then there is nothing for it; your crew must go overboard wearing buoyancy aid or lifejacket and attach a line with a bowline under his armpits so that he can be hauled aboard, effecting mouth to mouth respiration as and if necessary. (See Chapter Four.)

That is the worst situation you are ever likely to find yourself called upon to deal with. Keep a cool head, and when he is aboard assess the position with regard to the other chap. Is he all right for the time being? If he is, then your duty is to get the first man ashore immediately so that proper medical attention can be given, in the meantime your crew must continue to give artificial respiration. If you decide this is the course to take, throw the other chap a lifejacket if he hasn't got one and tell him you'll be back as soon as possible.

But now assume that all is well with them both and they are clinging to the swamped dinghy. First make quite sure where the mast, ropes of all description and any floating gear is in relation to the dinghy. It will almost certainly be trailing up wind of the boat acting as a drogue on the hull which is catching the wind. Make your final approach from down wind, so that all this trailing paraphernalia is away the other side the dinghy and clear of your propeller, otherwise you will probably foul some rope or sail underwater which immobilises you, too. Do not steer straight for the boat, because you are not trying to actually come into contact with her. If you do, the chances are you will do some damage to either her or your boat, or worse still one of the chaps in the water if he happens to get in between both. Steer so as to just come clear of her as illustrated in Figure 21. Get them both aboard by throwing each of them a line in turn, and see that the line is properly attached to them before they leave the dinghy to join you in the powerboat. Disengage your propeller before they are alongside.

After that it is just a matter of weighing up the situation with regard to the dinghy. If the chaps you have rescued want you to tow the dinghy ashore, then it must be done very very gently and at slow speed, otherwise whatever fitting your towline has been made fast to aboard her may simply pull out, or the entire section of the hull tear away: remember the resistance of a swamped boat is phenomenal. You may easily be towing a ton of trapped water in her hull, and it is our old friend inertia again. You have to get it on the move gently, and guide it gently when it is moving.

The best position to effect the tow is of course from your stern to her bow, but rarely is a sailing dinghy fitted with any adequate fairlead to keep the towrope at the stemhead—which is where it needs to be kept—and the temptation is always to make the line fast round the forestay near deck level. This generally results in the point of tow being rapidly transferred to threequarters of the way up the mast, which is the worst possible position to effect a tow, because the stemhead plate has ripped off. Isn't it fun?

Still: provided no other conditions are making the attempt dangerous to anyone's life, try you must, and the best word of advice I can leave you with is to do it all very gently, and remember that towrope is just yearning to get wrapped around your propeller. We will now deal with taking a normally floating boat in tow: a much more satisfactory operation.

TOWING ANOTHER CRAFT FROM A POWERBOAT

It is generally recognised that the craft about to be towed should supply the towline, but it does not always turn out that way. Your own berthing lines, or as a last resort your own anchor warp may have to be used, though the latter is a rather risky

WIND

*Figure 21*

*Correct way to approach capsized sailing dinghy when help is
required from a powerboat*

manoeuvre—you may wish to anchor yourself. Approach the craft to be towed from up wind, so as to give her a lee if possible. She should have fenders out on her weather side in case you end up alongside her, but this should not be necessary unless some member of the crew wishes to transfer to your boat to assist in the proceedings. There is another reason why it is generally best to approach from the windward side: if she casts her towrope to you and the rope falls short, her leeway—her drift through the water through wind resistance—will cause the rope to trail out upwind toward you. You can manoeuvre your craft so as to gain the end of the rope without having to go alongside her. Of course if she is anchored this will not apply.

Having gained your end of the towing warp, haul a few feet of it aboard and ask them to make their end fast in such a fashion that they can, if need be, cast it off while under strain. A couple of round turns on a samson post, or the mast, with the warp led through a fairlead at the stem and the end kept in hand will do. You then make fast your end by some similar means—a bowline with slip will suffice. If you have a crew, get them to keep the warp in hand and just taut without actually hauling the two boats into contact as he, or you, make fast the end of the rope. This is to ensure that the rope cannot get foul of your propeller. Check that the towrope is in fact leading through her fairlead or some other adequate device as near to her stemhead as possible and indicate to the crew of the towed craft that you now propose taking the strain. Do so easily so as not to snatch the warp viciously but to allow the other craft to gather way gently. Your crew can help greatly here by taking part of the strain on the warp himself, easing it out until the bowline takes the weight. This will have the effect of not only orientating the towed craft's bow towards you, but your own stern toward her before ever the main strain comes on the warp.

If the boat you are towing is small, such as a sailing dinghy, ask the crew to get fairly well aft—this makes her less liable to 'range' wildly to either side. In fact, if they for any reason come right forward in a small boat they may well dig the bow, causing the boat to range wildly and even capsize, since suddenly the point of tow is above and out of line with the keel and centre of gravity of the craft being towed. If it is a sailing dinghy ensure that they have lifted the centreplate right up, and ask them to man the tiller so as to keep her steady astern of you. Ensure that your crew keeps his eye on the towed craft all the time, or if you are alone give them a very frequent look yourself. Things can happen back there that you may not be aware of, and you do not always hear a shout above your own engine sound and the wind. This is why it is so essential that BOTH ends of the towrope can be easily cast off even while under tension if need be.

On approaching your destination you must remember that the craft astern is more or less at your mercy with regard to the momentum she is carrying and you should try to arrange it that she 'clews up' alongside at a speed within the capabilities of her crew to handle. They won't thank you if they damage themselves by ramming a jetty—and they have no brakes! Mind you a quick-witted crew could use a bucket attached to a lanyard with great advantage here.

YOU tell THEM when to cast off the towline and recover this into your boat otherwise (should you have cast off from your end) it will fall into the water ahead of the boat being towed and can foul anything either beneath their craft or on the bottom. For the sake of continuing good relations remember to return the tow-rope afterwards.

In a tideway it may be more convenient to keep them in tow until they are actually alongside the jetty or mooring, since you can adjust your own speed so that they are stationary relative to the object whatever it is. In this case it is essential that they do cast you free as soon as they have a headrope fast themselves otherwise it's quite possible for your boat, secured as she is by the stern, to get into a very awkward position at the end of that towrope athwart the run of the tide. You will need to cast off quickly from your end if this occurs.

To summarise, the important thing is to be able to cast off the tow from either end at any time, to take up the strain very easily and not be tempted to tow too fast, and to keep a good watch on the towed craft at all times.

## SMALL POWERBOATS OFF AN EXPOSED COASTLINE

Finally, should small highspeed or lowspeed power craft ever undertake a coastal passage? The answer is of course yes;

PROVIDED IT IS UNDERTAKEN WITH PROPER FORETHOUGHT with full cognizance of weather—present and coming—distances involved between safe points of refuge, state of the sea, and proximity of other craft in company together with due notification of some responsible authority ashore of one's exact intentions. It is always, naturally, a greater risk to embark on a coastal passage alone; if power failure occurs there is much to be said for a companion in another boat to give a tow!

The two main dangers along an exposed coast for such boats are engine failure and rapid deterioration in the weather. Dealing with the former first, remember that in a small highspeed powerboat it is not possible in anything of a 'chop' out at sea to effectively row or paddle when the engine fails. For this reason one should always carry a small auxiliary outboard which can be shipped quickly in case of need. If you have to resort to paddle or oars you will find that the hull shape is just not capable of responding to a feeble thrust from one side only, or alternate sides with a single paddle, and it is almost as unresponsive to a pair of oars. Everything is wrong. To begin with, more often than not, the engine is heavy and right aft and the propeller is the only unit of the whole hull which is deep enough in the water to grip, either in or out of action. The wind takes immediate charge once the engine has stopped, and nearly always blows the bow (which is riding high) down to leeward. There she is likely to stay with the deeper immersed stern and propeller unit acting as a drogue so that she gaily drifts down wind despite your efforts with the paddle or what-have-you. Which is bad enough, but let it happen in a roughening sea condition and it can quickly become dangerous because the low after end of the boat is now presented to the breaking waves which may be slopping all over the outboard you are frantically trying to restart—probably having removed the cover to check the plug or suchlike.

Get an anchor out from your bow if you can reach the bottom. If it is too deep make an improvised sea anchor from your floorboards, seat, the wife's picnic basket (See Chapter Eight) and secure the warp to your bow as soon as possible. Do everything you can to prevent drifting on shore or away from your nearest place of refuge. If your main power unit remains dud you will now have a breathing space to get the auxiliary motor operating.

Best of all, of course, is to have it permanently in the 'ready' position, but this is not always possible in the smaller craft.

In a conventionally shaped low power launch, engine failure is not quite such an immediate emergency unless you happen to be a few yards off a lee shore! The same precautions should be taken of course, but the margin of safety is greater here because the boat will not be quite so much at the mercy of the sea, being deeper draught and designed for floating 'in' and making way 'through' rather than sitting 'on' and making way 'over' the water as in the former case. She will be more amenable to rowing with a good pair of adequately long oars, and will not suffer from that excessively low transom which is really the bane of small highspeed power craft. Nevertheless, even in a slow speed conventional power launch an auxiliary power unit is advisable if tackling a coastal trip or even a day's jaunt out and back again to the starting point.

This is a seamanlike precaution and in these small power craft, fast or otherwise, it is wise to always have at the back of one's mind that one has, at minimum, so many minutes at normal speed back to safe refuge. It is enlightening how distance in terms of time can present an alarming aspect when visibility clamps down suddenly, or a rapid wind increase with its immediate roughening of the sea takes place. The minimum equipment which ought to be carried in any boat undertaking a coastal trip is dealt with under the appropriate sections in Chapters Four, Six and Seven.

Deteriorating weather, as the foregoing remarks imply, is a much greater hazard in a speedboat than in a conventionally shaped craft and assuming now that the power unit continues to operate let us think about the best action to take when in the former craft faced with a rapidly rising sea. Again, from the point of view of riding the seas these hulls are all wrong. Flattish underneath with no keel or ballast to keep the weight down low and grip the water, they can neither operate at the speed for which they are intended, nor are they capable of coping with the conditions at low speed. If your safe refuge is to windward, while the seas are still manageable, one should reduce speed compatible with maintaining control and try to take the crests of the bigger waves head on at a speed which precludes flying into the trough beyond. With the passing of one crest under the boat, open throttle and ease her across, but at all costs avoid presenting her beam to the crests because the breaking tops may easily shove the bow (which is light and high) down wind and put you stern on to the broken water. You must decide what is your best speed to take the waves with maximum safety, and nurse the boat into the seas as carefully as possible.

If the safe refuge lies down wind it is up to you to decide whether your craft can cope with overshooting the seas and presenting her stern to the breaking crests without danger of pooping. Within limits the faster you go here the less the danger of taking one in at the stern—but how fast can you go in such conditions without starting to leap off the backs of the waves like a ski-jumper?

Make no mistake, your best course of action is NOT to be out in such conditions in this type of craft.

The slow speed launch with conventional hull is a much safer proposition when things get rougher. Much the same considerations apply—she should be nursed into the breakers if the refuge lies to windward, and be prevented from broaching across the seas, but she will be much easier to handle due to the better grip in the water and better weight distribution toward the centre of the craft rather than concentrated right aft.

The decision whether to run before the seas or keep her headed into them will depend largely on the type of stern. If she has a good buoyant stern with adequate freeboard, Norwegian type or with a counter, then she will be almost as happy running before the seas as punching into them, but the speed to avoid is that which synchronises with the wave velocity. Keep her speed well below the wave speed so that they do not hang about under your stern and start the boat surfing. If necessary tow a couple of warps astern to dampen down the breaking crests and slow your own speed while maintaining control with the rudder.

If the boat has a fairly low freeboard aft, and a square transom, you may well choose to punch your way to windward rather than run off before the seas, even though the place of refuge may be somewhat farther than one down wind. If things get altogether too bad for this, the alternative is indicated in Chapter Eight under 'sea anchors'.

When planning a coastal trip, no matter what type of craft you are operating, it is as well to try to arrange your track line so that at worst you are never more than half an hour away from your nearest selected place of shelter.

. . .

Much that we have considered regarding the small powerboat will of course equally apply to the sailing dinghy so far as precautions when going coastwise are concerned. As I mentioned before, my intention here is not to teach a reader how to sail, but to survey the situations which call for that 'little more' by way of expertise than just the normal handling of a dinghy.

SAILING DINGHIES IN COASTAL WATERS

It is important to understand that once the great majority of sailing dinghies have left sheltered water, or that area of sea which is within immediate reach of shelter, they are operating in an environ for which they were not specifically designed.

I will repeat that it is just here that the design of the majority of dinghies parts company with the requirements of a true seaboat. A craft under sail which will carry her way and gain to windward in a sea must have a good length, adequate draught, weight and freeboard, and a fine bow which will not be stopped unduly by the punch of a steep wave. Most sailing dinghies are constructed as lightly as possible compatible with strength of hull, and with a shape which is geared to give speed in flat water. They tend therefore to be thrown about and stopped dead by a short steep sea.

We have broadly surveyed the requirements by way of shape for a good seaboat: measure your dinghy against those yardsticks and you will have a fair assessment as to whether she will be happy in anything of a sea. Know your boat and don't ask her to perform feats which are outside her capabilities, no matter how expert you may be in handling her.

There are dinghies which do go a long way toward approaching the difficult compromise between a comparatively light, high performance boat and a good seaboat. The sixteen foot Wayfarer is one which comes to mind, and the eighteen foot Drascombe Lugger (chosen for the cruise in Chapter Seven) was designed specifically for coping with open sea conditions. I mention only two. There are others on the market and you will find that they all have these primary qualities; a fair amount of freeboard, a good rise to the bow and a nice curve along the keel from the stem to a buoyant stern. Remember that the rapidly rising wind (which has the effect of a short fetch) brings from the start just those steep, short waves which will bring the small lightly constructed hull to a standstill.

The carvel and hot or cold moulded laminate hull (and its counterpart in glassfibre) will be faster but wetter than the clinker or shiplapped hull at sea. This is because it offers little impediment to the rise of the water upward at the bow, and some of it comes inboard. But it is good for slicing cleanly through small waves.

A clinker hull, because of the overlapping plank edges, does tend to offer more resistance to forward motion at the bow, but at the same time she does throw the water away from the hull skin in doing so, and is therefore somewhat drier, though a little slower in a sea.

The plywood or fibreglass single and double chine hull will slap the water badly in waves unless carefully fined away in a deep 'V' toward the stem. In this respect the Wayfarer has a splendid bow for buoyancy and cleaving through the waves but she is a wet boat because the chines forward merge so well into a smooth bow such as one finds in the carvel or moulded hulls. This is good for allowing the boat to cleave a way through a wave, but it does little to prevent the spray lifting as it slaps against the weather bow—back comes the wetting (but not dangerously green) top of it over the jib handler!

Be under no illusion here; if you want exciting racing with the local club, and enjoy speed on the water for speed's sake and the thrilling response of a lively hull and immaculately tailored sails, don't ask the sort of boat you own to go out and risk having to cope with a rising sea off an exposed coastline.

The main point to remember when handling a dinghy in relatively rough water and brisk wind is to nurse her along, rather than try to drive her hard. This way you will keep her a lot drier and put much less strain on her gear. Keep her as upright as possible and don't allow water to accumulate in her as this will make her sluggish and more liable to take it 'green'.

You should practise handling her in such conditions when there is a safe lee within easy reach, before ever setting off on a hop down the coast, because it takes one time to 'feel' the boat in these different circumstances. When on the wind, avoid 'pinching' at all costs, for a steep sea can stop her dead and get you in irons. At the same time you must avoid getting too much way on through paying off: it is a critical and stimulating interplay of the boat's requirements and your responses. The area of water which concerns you most when close hauled is that which lies immediately on your weather bow, and you should watch it like a hawk, gathering way when possible in the flatter patches, and easing her bow up a little into the larger waves while making sure you retain steerage way.

It may well be that due to the tidal stream and wind direction you find she is drier on one tack than the other: if possible it is sense to make your long boards on the drier tack. When you decide to tack, wait for the right moment: tack during one of the 'flatter' patches of water, for if the boat is caught by a larger wave just at the moment when she is going through the wind with the power off, she may well be headed, and either miss stays or be put in irons. It will not matter a great deal if she is, provided you and your crew realise the fact and balance the boat exactly as required when she again takes the wind in her sails. Remember it is at that moment that the greatest likelihood of a capsize takes place, for the heeling effect is strongest since the craft is not moving through the water.

When sailing off the wind you will, of course, move your weight farther aft and adjust your centreboard so that it is about one quarter down: I do not recommend ever having it right up in these rough conditions (except when 'surfing' on a wave—more later). The reason for this is twofold. It is a distinct advantage to have a 'pivot point' in the form of some definite centre of lateral resistance forward of your rudder when the boat is being 'bounced' down wind. It gives far more positive rudder response. The second reason is that in the unfortunate event of a capsize you have the tip of the plate already showing out of the centreboard case—it saves a lot of mucking about in the cockpit before you can even begin to right the boat, struggling to push or pull the plate down so that you can use it as a lever to get her upright again.

Try to avoid sailing directly down wind: the chances of a gybe are greatly increased by the yawing of the boat. But if you do and you wish to change tacks, you may well, and wisely, decide to bring her on the wind, put about, and free off on the other tack to a run again, rather than gybe. It is too easy for a gybe to result in violent broaching across the wind when in lumpy sea conditions, and this frequently results in a capsize.

If you are finding, even after reefing your main that she is over pressed, drop your foresail and stow it if sailing on the wind. Drop the main if running, and keep her sailing under foresail alone, provided you can make your safe refuge on such a course —and this may not necessarily be the destination for which you set off. When things have got to this stage you should aim for the nearest lee where you may safely beach and get ashore. Then let those who are concerned know that you are safe: they will be worrying about you.

In the final Chapter we shall think about action to take if ever caught at sea where any thought of beaching is out of the question. It is a nasty situation, and one in which, if you have acted properly beforehand, you never should find yourself. But it can happen.

Now let us give some thought to a few specific situations which call for seamanship in a sailing dinghy.

### RIGHTING A CAPSIZED DINGHY

The immediate thing to remember when involved in a capsize is to avoid becoming separated from the boat. She may be drifting down wind faster than you think, and it can take a strong swimmer to regain the craft. The next most important matter is to avoid, if at all possible, allowing the boat to turn turtle with the mast plumbing the depths. In shallow water the mast will almost certainly be badly strained or bent, and anyway the boat is much easier to right from a 'flat on her side' position with the sails and mast lying along the surface of the water.

If you have a crew, get him or her to work along to the bow and simply hold on to the forestay at deck level, then, using the centreboard as a lever either by pressing on it gently with your foot (if you are on top of the boat) or pulling down with your arms (if you are in the water) bring the boat upright. She will immediately swing head-to-wind due to the drogue action of your crew holding on to the stem.

It is then up to you to embark over the transom (so as to avoid capsizing her again as you get in) and start shovelling the water out. When she is fully buoyant again help your crew to the stern and get him aboard, but this has to be done very quickly otherwise his drogue effect at the stern will allow the boat to pay off from the wind and start sailing while he is struggling to get aboard.

You will notice that in the above detail I have not mentioned dropping the sails, and this is because in most modern dinghies with their adequate buoyancy, it is a simple matter to right them and bail dry in a minute or so while luffed-up and sails set. If, however, your craft is not too liberally endowed with buoyancy and it is obviously going to take some time to get her sailing again, or if perhaps the strength of wind is such that there would be a chance of immediate capsize as soon as she is righted, bring both main and jib down before righting her. This is not always quite as easy as it sounds, particularly if the halyards have not been stowed neatly and are wrapped round every other bit of equipment in the boat! Which will just serve to teach you that ALL free ends of halyards and warps should at ALL times be neatly coiled and secured in a boat. Ensure that your crew remains at the bow until you are satisfied that the boat is ready to sail again, and when using the centreboard, remember it will not take the weight of a heavy man jumping on its extremity! Lever it gently. If you are alone in the boat, get the sails down before attempting to right her, or you may well capsize her again before you have bailed her dry. *And remember, don't get separated from the boat.*

GOING TO THE RESCUE UNDER SAIL

The difference in principle between carrying out a rescue under power and sail is that, in the latter case, you are only concerned with the crew of the boat in trouble; you should not concern yourself at all with recovering the craft, except perhaps for notifying some power launch that she needs a tow in. Never try to tow a waterlogged or capsized craft by means of a sailing dinghy. By the nature of things your dinghy has got to be allowed to respond to the wind. If she is prevented from doing so—by a taut towline—unless you are very experienced indeed, the dinghy will take matters into her own hands and put you all in the water.

Most dinghy sailors manage to right a capsized dinghy within seconds or minutes, taking the mainsail down—and the jib as well if need be—while she is still capsized to make things easier if conditions demand. However, on the rare occasion they may be quite unable to get her sailing, and it is your duty to go to their assistance even though you are yourself under sail. The procedure I would suggest is as follows.

In water which is shallow enough for you to anchor, and assuming that there is no strong tideway, sail up wind of the capsize and drop and secure the foresail. Have some line ready to heave to the capsized boat, and get your own anchor ready for letting go. Sail just down wind of the lame boat and round up head to wind so as to carry way up close to, and across wind from her at the same time heaving your line across, directing her crew to make it fast to her bow—through the fairlead and round the mast will do. You at the same time drop your anchor. The capsized dinghy will be drifting with the wind astern of you, and provided you are sure your anchor is holding you can now drop your mainsail.

Often, under this condition, it will become possible for the lame dinghy to be righted and bailed out, to carry on sailing under her own power. If this proves impossible transfer her crew aboard your craft and sail them to shore, first making your anchor warp fast to the still capsized or swamped boat. Be sure to take them aboard over your transom, and in this respect a short 'bight' of line made from your own mainsheet will prove invaluable for them to get a leg up.

If the water is too deep for you to anchor, forget about trying to right the lame dinghy and concentrate on getting her crew aboard your boat. Sail across the wind two or three boats' lengths to leeward of the lame boat, rounding up head-to-wind so as to carry your way gently up close to her stern. Cast a line to them, and get them to pass the end round their sheethorse or some other fitting from which it can easily unreeve, then cast the end back to you. Put both parts through your own fairlead at the stem and make them fast. You are now secured head-to-wind,

94

using her as a sea anchor. Drop your sails. Pass another line to her crew, and see that they make it fast round themselves before leaving their boat to be hauled back to your own transom and aboard. It is important that this line is made fast round himself by the chap in the water, for if through any reason after they have left their own boat they get cramp or have a heart attack—and it does happen in cold water—they may very quickly be left up wind by the two boats, both of which will be drifting to leeward.

When all are safely aboard, free one end of your bow line allowing it to unreeve from the other boat, and sail back to shore.

You may wonder why I advise dropping your sails since your craft is luffed up head-to-wind anyway. Two reasons: the jibsheets can easily become foul and cause the jib to fill, thus swinging her head off the wind which will start her sailing and probably result in your crashing into the lame boat, and secondly when the chaps are coming in over the transom they do not want their fingers chopped off by a viciously sliding sheethorse traveller. Neither do you want your head clouted by the boom while you are assisting them aboard. Things are much easier with the sails down: you have time to think.

BEING TAKEN IN TOW WHEN ABOARD A SAILING CRAFT

As soon as the towing craft is near, round up head-to-wind and drop your sails. Leave the rudder shipped and see that the tiller is free to steer. Raise the centreboard, and if you have any fenders put them out over your weather side. Have your towing warp ready to sling across and call her alongside to weather of you so that she provides a lee. Pass the coil of warp forward of the shroud before heaving it to her. Make the inboard end fast so that it can quickly be cast off, even under strain. Ask her to take up the slack and take the strain easily, trimming your own craft down by the stern and steering her so as to follow inside her wake.

If the towing craft stops and is evidently waiting for you to sail alongside so as to pass the towing warp, always do so to leeward of her, and get your sails down immediately the warp is secure on both craft.

### ANCHORING A SAILING CRAFT

Having ensured that the anchor and warp are cleared away to let go, drop the jib and round up head-to-wind. When you have almost lost way through the water drop your anchor, paying out enough warp to equal three times the depth of the water. When you are happy that the anchor is holding, drop your mainsail.

### REEFING A SLOOP UNDER WAY

Almost all modern sailing dinghies have roller-reefed mainsails, and it is a wise crew which reefs in plenty of time before conditions get difficult. The craft is then not only safer in strong winds, but faster also, since one does not have to either 'spill' wind or allow her to heel inefficiently.

Bring the craft on to Starboard tack. This is because your main halyard is cleated to Starboard—or should be—thus it is in a better position for your crew to work it.

Sail her close hauled, and let fly the mainsheet, cleating the jib so that your crew now has both hands free.

Ease the helm a little to leeward which will counteract the tendency of the boat to pay off the wind. Do not allow her to luff up.

Your crew can now 'start' the main halyard, and you can be assisting him from the after end of the cockpit by keeping her sailing on the wind by means of your knee at the tiller. After lowering the required amount of mainsail unship the boom from the gooseneck, roll the sail by rotating the boom, taking care that the leech is kept stretched well aft along the boom, and that the luffrope does not foul the hole for the gooseneck in the forward end of the boom. Re-house the boom on the gooseneck and hoist the main taut.

This is not at all easy to do in anything of a 'chop' when the boat is plunging wildly, so it pays to practice with your crew in these sort of conditions to get the feel of the whole thing. Find the lee of some high land before reefing if possible.

### TACTICAL SAILING IN NON-TIDAL WATERS

Unless you have practised racing your dinghy, the chances are that you have seldom been directly concerned with the shortest—

*Underwater lines of the new 48-foot 'Solent' class Royal National Lifeboat. The photograph shows the boat undergoing self-righting tests.*

*Fairey 'Spearfish' at speed, giving an indication of the shock pressures the high-speed hull must be capable of withstanding.*

*TERYLENE 8 plait (matt finish). 1¼″ cir-*
*cumference extensively used for dinghy*
*sheets. Minimum strength (standard): 31¼*
*cwt. Minimum strength (matt): 20 cwt.*

*ULSTRON 8 plait cover. 1¼″ circumfer-*
*ence extensively used for dinghy sheets.*
*Light green in colour. Minimum strength:*
*26¾ cwt.*

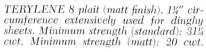

*5. Construction of synthetic rope and wire.*

*TERYLENE 3 strand. Extensively used*
*for anchor warps. Recommended sizes:*
*Craft 10–16 feet: ¾″ circ. Minimum*
*strength 11 cwt. Craft 18–22 feet: 1½″*
*circ. Minimum strength 44½ cwt.*

*Stainless steel wire rope. Extensively used*
*for standing rigging in small craft. ⅜″*
*circumference. 1 x 19 construction. Break-*
*ing strain with jerk load: 1680 lbs.*

and therefore sometimes the quickest—course to take from one point to another.

Assuming there to be no tide, let us imagine our destination to be up wind in such a position that we cannot lay it when close hauled on either tack. The problem presents itself: is it quicker, given a steady wind direction, to sail close hauled on one tack until the destination is just abaft the beam, then tack and make it on the second board, or carry out a series of short boards, tacking frequently? Or would it perhaps be better to sail somewhat free of the wind on a close reach, again until the destination is just abaft the beam before tacking, thus making it in two long but faster boards?

Figure 22 will make this clear.

Obviously, in terms of distance travelled, course A and A¹ will be identical, as will the time taken to effect them.

Course C, close hauled on a number of short boards with five tacks into the bargain, covers exactly the same distance through the water.

Course B, sailing somewhat freer of the wind 'full-and-by' covers a longer distance.

In terms of time however, course A and A¹ will take the same period.

Course C will take considerably longer because not only have you tacked five times quite unnecessarily—and the boat loses way on each tack momentarily—but you will probably, without realising it, start to 'pinch' her on that last board in order to make 'Y'. This too of course results in the boat moving more slowly.

Course B, on the other hand, even though over a greater distance will probably result in your getting to 'Y' before the boat on either A or A¹ because by sailing full-and-by you move so much faster than when sailing close hauled. It depends to a certain extent on one's boat: not all sailing boats show a marked improvement in performance between a beat (close hauled) and a close reach.

Appreciation of any wind shifts while to leeward of 'Y' is important, because any change from the existing state of affairs must tend to favour one tack and place one at a disadvantage on the other.

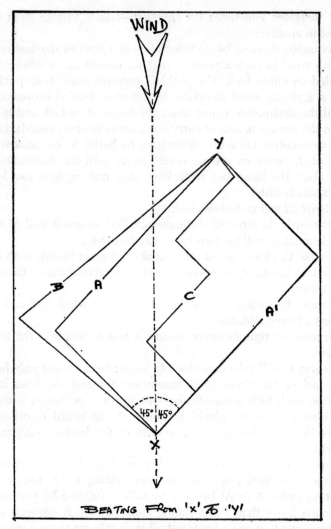

*Figure 22*

A, A¹ and C are the same distance
B is longer distance
A and A¹ take the same time
C takes longer
B though farther is often the quickest

# The Expertise of Boat Handling

This is interesting sport, for the situation can embrace an almost infinite number of either adverse or advantageous effects.

If you wish to calculate the effect on your speed and track over the bottom while sailing in a tideway, be aware that there is far more to it than the simple appreciation that a tidal stream will obviously affect your ability to make good a given point, and will call for a course allowance to be made. It depends on the relative direction not only of your course line to the run of the tide, but also of the relative angle between the run of the tide and the wind you are using. Remember that the wind you are using is not the wind that an observer in an anchored boat will feel: it is the wind affect on you WHO ARE IN TURN AFFECTED BY THE TIDAL STREAM. It's all a matter of relativity, and once that word enters into a problem, you can phone for a computer!

Basically though, you may easily imagine that with a cross wind and a tide from dead ahead, the speed a sailing boat will make over the bottom will be equal to her normal ground speed with the given wind force and no tide, LESS the speed of the tidal stream. If she would normally make six knots and the tide is completely adverse, running at two knots, then will she not be making four knots over the bottom?

Similarly, if the tidal stream is completely favourable, would she not, in the above wind circumstance, make good eight knots over the bottom?

Or would she? Did you agree with that assessment?

Think again. With no tide to affect her she would be making six knots in either direction, since the one is the reciprocal of the other and both are dead across the wind. But with a completely adverse tidal stream affecting her, her speed will be diminished over the bottom, and therefore the apparent wind in the boat will appear to come slightly more free—present a greater angle to the fore-and-aft line of the boat.

With a completely favourable tidal stream the speed over the bottom will be augmented, and the apparent wind changes will certainly affect her speed through the water—and therefore over the bottom.

So our original assumption that under this condition of tide and wind one simply has to either deduct or add the speed of the tide is quite wrong for a sailing boat. It would be perfectly all right for a powerboat, for she is not dependant on the wind speed or inclination to her fore-and-aft line for her motive power and resultant speed.

But now imagine the infinite variety of circumstances possible with different courses relative to the tidal stream, different tidal stream directions relative to the wind, and the resultant boat's motive power relative to both! I leave you to it: it can afford many a tortured evening with parallel rulers, protractors, calculation of vectors and prescription of sleeping pills.

Much the same problems must have been faced when calculating the resultant course of the Apollo space vehicles: the orbit of earth round sun, and moon round earth, would be equivalent on Apollo to the tide effect on our boat, while the inclination of the pressure of light would have been the equivalent to the wind effects. But they had a computer.

Only one thing is quite plain. If tidal stream and wind are directly opposed, then one's apparent wind in the boat will be the sum of both, provided you are stationary in relation to the water, and the difference of both when the wind and tide are together. Once one starts sailing however complex vectors enter into the problem.

In Chapter Two, we dealt in some detail with the reaction of tidal streams to headlands, promontories and bays, and the retarding effect of the banks of an estuary to the speed of flow.

In a sailing dinghy all these phenomena should be studied carefully, for they can easily make the difference between making good one's destination, or having to make a change of plans and go elsewhere.

Broadly speaking, just remember that it pays to study the shape of a coastline or estuary bank in detail should you find that you are stemming an adverse tide. There is generally some more advantageous tactic than the straightforward slog against the tide, bearing in mind the possibility of changed direction of wind along a cliff face, and slowing down or complete contra-running eddy of tide. It is pointless to say more than this: you must look for the obvious helps.

## HEAVING-TO IN A SAILING DINGHY

This is a means of keeping a boat, while under way, as nearly stationary as possible, and generally results, in a sloop rig, in making slight headway. The jib is sheeted hard aback—to weather—and the main eased with the helm slightly alee. What happens is that the jib forces the bow off the wind until the main grips the wind sufficiently to prevent any further paying off, bringing the bow back up into the wind, whereupon the jib is forced against the wind until the main again starts to spill wind, when the jib brings the bow off the wind again. It causes a 'see-saw' movement of the boat, although it is possible with experiment in a steady wind to get jib, main, helm and centreboard so correctly balanced and acting against each other that the boat will stay relatively motionless, making slight leeway.

You should practise this, and also practise steering the boat with the rudder unshipped, it's fascinating. Put the boat on to a reach, and unship the rudder and tiller. You will probably find you have to put the jib aback to prevent her tacking, and then by easing the jibsheet she will come on the wind, and by hardening jibsheet she will pay off the wind, provided the mainsheet is trimmed exactly right. You can make way through the water to a destination up wind, but you will never sail down wind with no rudder and the main set. If you want to try, drop your mainsail and use the jib alone: it's surprising too what can be done by a shift of the crew's weight to swing her bow to one side or the other of a line straight down wind.

## BEACHING A SAILING DINGHY THROUGH SURF ON A LEE SHORE

By surf we are thinking here of moderately small waves breaking on a sandy or shingle beach where there is no great danger of a swamping provided the situation is properly handled.

Never try to run on to a lee shore with sails set—at least certainly not with the main set. In calmish conditions when presenting one's stern to the seas is no hazard, it is quite acceptable to run in under jib, but get the rudder off her immediately she touches down, and round her up head-to-waves as soon as you jump out, then take her stern first up the beach.

In larger seas, you must round up head-to-wind while still

outside the line of the first breaking waves. If you have oars use them to keep her head-to-sea and unship the rudder, allowing the boat to drift stern first on to the beach. It is essential that she remains head-to-sea otherwise she may broach and capsize or fill with a breaker slamming her flat on the beam. When you jump out on touch-down DON'T STAND CLOSE TO THE BOAT ON HER SHOREWARD SIDE because you can get a nasty clout on the shins when the next breaker drives her a few feet back up the beach. Keep her head-to-sea and pull her as quickly as possible up the beach out of reach of the biggest surge.

If you have no oars or paddles, after rounding up and handing all sail, shove your bailing bucket out on the end of a line from the bow. This will act as an improvised sea anchor to keep her head-to-sea while she drifts in. You may be sure of one thing: those waves will be bigger on the beach than you expected!

The great thing is to be sure that you and your crew know exactly what you are about, and do whatever has to be done QUICKLY. Even if the boat is swamped—keep her head-to-sea at all cost otherwise she will become unmanageable. If the tide is falling and she has been swamped, you are in luck, for the sea is withdrawing which gives you a chance to get her emptied. Never simply leave the dinghy on the shore full of water, while waiting for the tide to fall: she will be badly strained by the weight of water inside her. Open the self-bailers, and bail her out by bucket to help hasten the process.

If the tide is rising you have problems! If there are enough of you present, stand all on one side of the swamped boat and, just as a series of waves withdraws, heave her bodily over as quickly as you can to empty the hull. Then, before the next surge of waves advances again, get her on a level keel and pull her back up the beach, assisted by the wave. She will be semi-buoyant now, and then you can get on with the job of bailing her dry. But it doesn't do the boat much good!

## BEACHING A SAILING DINGHY THROUGH SURF ON A WEATHER SHORE

With wind off shore the situation is more difficult, for although you must still drop all sail before getting within the line of breaking waves, you will have to use the oars to both keep her

102

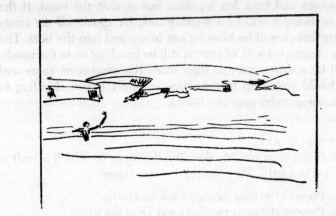

YOUR VIEW OF HER

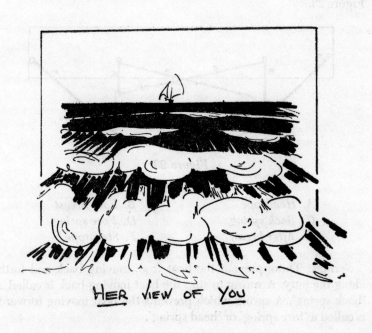

HER VIEW OF YOU

head-to-sea and back her in, stern first against the wind. If the wind is strong it will be a wetting task, for spume off the crests near the beach will be blowing out to sea and into the boat. The waves themselves will, of course, still be breaking on to the beach. It will be a slower process than when the wind is on shore and you should weigh up the situation carefully before deciding to try a landing under such conditions.

. . .

BERTHING WARPS

This is the term used to describe the ropes by which a craft is made fast to a jetty. They should do three things:

1. Prevent the boat moving back and forth.
2. Prevent the craft moving away from the jetty.
3. Allow the craft to move up and down the jetty with the rise and fall of the tide.

In larger boats three sets of lines are used to do this: they are called 'springs', 'head and sternropes' and 'breastropes'. See Figure 23.

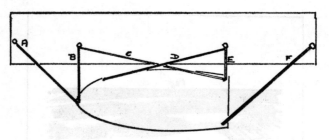

*Figure 23*

*Berthing Warps*

| | |
|---|---|
| A. *Headrope* | B. *Fore breast* |
| C. *Back spring* | D. *Fore spring* |
| E. *After breast* | F. *Sternrope* |

*Springs:* These prevent the boat from moving back and forth along the jetty. A spring to stop the boat moving back is called a 'back spring'. A spring which prevents the boat moving forward is called a 'fore spring' or 'head spring'.

*Headropes and sternropes:* These assist the springs in keeping the boat in a given position adjacent to the jetty, and in addition take some of the strain off the springs when a strong stream is running.

*Breastropes:* These run more or less at right angles from near the bow (fore breast), and stern (after breast), to the jetty, and govern the distance away from the jetty that the boat can ride. In a small boat they also hold her upright when she takes the bottom.

It will be evident that where a rise and fall of tide has to be catered for, these ropes will either require constant tending, being shortened as the tide rises and lengthened as the tide falls, or else will have to be left slack enough to cater for the maximum fall of tide that can take place while they are unattended—most particularly the breastropes if rigged.

Often, in small boats, a headrope and sternrope is sufficient, since these two ropes partly do the jobs of both springs and breastropes, and also provide the big advantage that with a varying height of tide and reciprocal running directions of the stream, they effectively keep the boat in against the jetty whichever one of them is in use—the sternrope with a stream running under her stern, and the headrope when it is running under her bow.

PRECAUTIONS WHEN MAKING FAST ALONGSIDE

Always allow enough slack to cater for the fall or rise of tide should you propose leaving the boat unattended for any length of time.

Check on the nature of the bottom beneath your craft before leaving her if she is to 'take the ground'. It may be that there is a sharp incline (there often is against a jetty) which would be enough to dip her gunwale under when the rising tide returns! Also, are there any sharp boulders, stones, broken bottles or old bicycles and washing machines down there?

Check that she cannot in any way become lodged, with the rising tide, beneath any projection in the face of the jetty. I once berthed a ship alongside a jetty at high tide when all was clear. As the tide fell, however, the ship moved vertically down the jetty until her deck level was beneath a protruding beam running horizontally along the jetty face. With the rising tide the gunwale firmly jammed beneath this beam—a fact which gradually made itself known to all by an increasing angle of heel! It all took place with utmost stealth and silence! By the time we had discovered the cause—we were all thinking we had sprung a leak—the pressure under that beam withstood every attempt to prise her free. What would you have done?

We didn't need to! With a frightful rending the whole beam suddenly tore out of its fastenings and the ship nearly capsized the opposite way. It was very bad seamanship to allow this to happen, but I'm glad the beam was not immovable otherwise I dread to think what might have resulted. Remember this: don't ever leave your boat beneath a jetty with any projections at Low Water. You may think you will be back within five minutes, but things can happen ashore that prevent you!

Thinking on these lines, it is never really very satisfactory to leave a boat actually in contact with a jetty for long periods, even though she is free to ride up and down. All sorts of things can happen: a large ship may pass and her displacement wake will slop your boat violently every way, sometimes parting fender lines or nudging them up over the gunwale into the boat so that she is left unprotected grating against the rough jetty face, to the detriment of your paintwork. It is often more seamanlike to drop an anchor out in deep water and moor her with a head or stern-line ashore so that she rides clear of all obstructions.

If she is to be left for long periods, it may be possible to arrange it so that the headrope is led through a block suspended from some height. By securing a weight to the end of the headrope the boat is constantly pulled away from the shore or jetty, while being free to rise and fall with the tide, or be pulled ashore for boarding. See Figure 24.

If berthing alongside another yacht, remember it is your job to put adequate fenders out on your own craft to eliminate any chafe to his hull, and never use his berthing warps to take the weight of your own craft: why should you? Get your own head-rope and sternrope ashore—he can always slip out from inside you if he wants to by passing them round himself as he slides away. If he is as courteous as you, he might even remember to put your warps back to the jetty!

Remember too that even though the harbour master may have

MARVELLOUS SIGHT — THESE REALLY BIG 'UNS
GOING FAST...

directed you to berth alongside another boat, it is courtesy to hail her and request permission before actually doing so. When you eventually go ashore do so across her foredeck and not across her cockpit area—it's a matter of respecting another craft's privacy.

*Figure 24*

*Holding a dinghy off a quay wall*
*To prevent damage to boat, pass the painter through a block slung from any convenient point away from the jetty and attach a weight to the end. The boat is thus pulled away from the wall to which a sternline is attached, and allowance is made for the rise and fall of the tide.*

BEACHWORK

One of the hazards to small craft left on a tidal beach is the difference in range between Neaps and Springs. Frequently a boat pulled well up a sloping beach above Neap High Water will float as the tides start to make up to Springs. Remember, too, if you value the paint on your dinghy or launch, that it is not good enough just to calculate where High Water Springs will reach and pull her bow up above that line. With the increasing High Water lines along the beach every other boat which may be anchored on the beach (if it is a lee shore) will float to the High Water line. At the top of the tides when there is very little beach left there will be an accumulation of craft, often far too close to one another, juggling about and nudging each other to the detriment of their appearance and the good relations of their owners.

It pays, if leaving a boat for any time, to pull her well up above High Water Springs, and then from the water point of view she is safe. You still have to think of wind, however, and a small light dinghy with a tall mast can easily be capsized on dry land. Orientate her head into the prevailing wind direction, and if she is to be left for long it is worth asking a local boatman or boat-yard to keep an eye on her for a suitable remuneration. Owners sometimes sink weights into the sand or shingle, with eyes attached to which a lanyard can be secured after passing over the hull and this is an excellent idea provided one has permission from the owner of the beach, and can more or less stake one's claim to any particular section of it: remember the foreshore is more often than not free for all to use.

Digging a hollow and putting your craft into this, with the sand piled up against either side is another way of preventing blowing over. The trouble here is that with a continuous strong wind all the sand will blow from round the boat and the wind will gradually dig the hole deeper and allow her to sink down. It scours the sand from under the bow and stern, piling it high in another area, and often one can return to find the boat herself completely buried under a drift.

Though small power launches are less liable to capsize by wind on a sandy beach, they are subject to this latter burying tendency, and in addition the fine dust and grit which blows at a height of a few inches above the beach level will penetrate into any machinery left on board. It is the worst thing possible for outboard motors and certainly these should be either removed or well protected from the sand blast.

If you put an anchor out—and it is advisable even though the boat may be above High Water—always bury it well otherwise somebody may trip on it and injure themselves.

It is worthwhile to have a stout cover—twelve ounce water-proofed canvas is good for this—made to fit snugly over the whole upper part of the boat, to keep dust, sand and grit out of her, but be aware of the following if you do.

When a cover is put over any craft there should be provision for a free flow of air beneath it, otherwise the interior will become foul due to the dampness being trapped. P.V.C. (Polyvinyl coated) covers are worse than canvas for this, as they allow no 'breathing' whatever, and I have often taken one such from over a dinghy in hot sunshine to be met with a hot dank smell of wet, and everything in the boat was soaked due to the fact that the humidity in the atmosphere had been unable to evaporate. They are a mixed blessing, and my own feeling is that unless one can so arrange it that there is this flow of air, without of course allowing the rain in, then perhaps a boat may be better left without any form of cover provided any water which enters can flow out again through drain holes. At least she keeps sweet.

GROUND TACKLE

There are two methods of securing a craft to the bottom while still afloat: anchoring and mooring. The former allows full swing with the change of the tide or wind, while the latter allows very little swing. Both call for adequate ground tackle.

There are three main anchors in use by small boats today; the oldest is known as the Admiralty pattern, or Fisherman anchor as illustrated in Figure 25. In fact, this is very much older than the Admiralty being in use in the time of the Phoenicians. It consists of the shank, at the lower end of which is attached a curved bar carrying the flukes; a removable stock slides through the top of the shank in the opposite plane to the flukes. This stock, when removed, slides through the shank until it comes up towards its curved end which allows it to fall down and stow neatly alongside the shank. Before using this type of anchor, the stock has to be locked into the position shown in the illustration with a retaining pin and when dropped on to the bottom the stock then ensures that as soon as a horizontal pull comes on the anchor, it will fall over so that one of the flukes digs in.

This anchor has good holding power on all but rock, but suffers the great disadvantage of one fluke being permanently above the level of the bottom. With the turn of the tide, your anchor warp can easily wrap itself around this fluke, thereby rendering the anchor virtually useless when the pull of the boat comes on it since it is being pulled out as it were instead of digging in to the

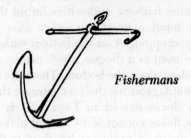

*Fishermans*

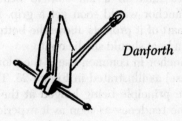

*Danforth*

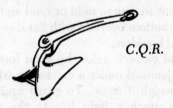

*C.Q.R.*

### Figure 25

### Three main types of small boat anchors

bottom. In addition it is possible for your own boat or somebody else's to impale herself on the exposed fluke as she dries out and for this reason some harbour authorities forbid their use. It has, however, to my mind a great advantage over other types of anchor in that by dropping it on the bottom without the stock in position it can be used as a drogue which can by a sufficient pull be persuaded to drag along the bottom. There are occasions when this is a great advantage as we shall see later on the cruise.

The Danforth demonstrated in Figure 25 is a more recent design where the flukes consist of two metal plates hinged at the lower end of the shank. Also the stock is fixed to the lower end of the shank and when the anchor is pulled along the bottom the flukes or palms drop down to dig in thereby tending to bury both themselves and the stock. It is excellent for use in soft sand or mud but sometimes fails on a flat shingle beach where the Admiralty pattern anchor would soon get a grip. It has the big advantage that no part of it projects above the bottom sufficiently to cause damage to a boat should she lie on it.

A third type of anchor in common use is the plough or C.Q.R. (coastal quick release) as illustrated in Figure 25. This makes use of the plough share principle being hinged at the lower end of the shank so that the tendency as soon as it experiences a pull is for the plough share point to dig into the bottom. As soon as this happens, it has a self-righting effect which immediately increases the tendency to dig deep. Once this has got a grip it is claimed to have twice the holding power of an Admiralty pattern anchor and again it is excellent for use in mud or sand and loose shingle but tends to fail on a bottom overlaid with flat disc-like stones or sizeable near-spherical boulders.

No anchor will hold on rock unless by good fortune the fluke or plough share gets jammed under a crevice, in which case you probably will never weigh it again. To guard against this latter eventuality, one can attach a light line to the crown of the anchor, buoying the line when the anchor is laid. In the event of becoming fouled, a pull on this line is often enough to dislodge it, but in practice in the tideway, I have usually found that the buoy line and the anchor warp become inextricably snarled up with each other and this can be conducive to reducing the efficient hold of the anchor.

For dinghies and other craft up to eighteen feet in length, anchors of from eight to sixteen pounds in weight will give adequate holding.

For very small pram dinghies, the grapnel is sufficient of two or three pounds weight. It has poor holding, is a menace to stow since the points are always exposed, but is extremely useful for dragging along the bottom to recover a lost chain or warp, though I would advise attaching a light line to its crown for dislodging it, in case you hook something that you are unable to lift.

Anchoring is of course a temporary method of securing your boat to the seabed and while the efficiency of an anchor is directly proportional to its shape and weight, both these factors are severely limited by the fact that it has to be lifted into the boat and stowed therein.

### ANCHORING A BOAT

Regardless of what type of anchor you are using, you should always try to pay out at least three times the depth of water on the anchor warp. This, of course, means three times the depth at High Water. The more upward is the pull on your anchor, the more chance it has of dragging.

Ideally the last couple of fathoms or so of your anchor warp should be chain cable—quarter inch galvanised is a useful size for small boats. This is for two reasons. Firstly, it ensures by its own weight that any upward pull from the boat is absorbed as it were by the weight of the chain cable so that when the strain comes on the anchor itself it will be only in a horizontal plane thereby enabling the anchor to dig and get a good grip on the bottom. Secondly, the movement of the boat both vertically with the surface motion and horizontally with change of tide or variations of the wind will tend to chafe your anchor warp where in contact with the bottom. You will appreciate that this chafe will be worst down near the anchor where your warp will be in contact continuously with the seabed. So you see, it is a wise precaution to have this chafe area taken by cable rather than synthetic or natural rope fibres. You will soon notice, if you have no chain adjacent to your anchor, how the warp becomes furry more particularly at the thimble eye where it is shackled to the anchor

113

ring bolt. The shoulder of this eye tends to get the full brunt of the chafe on the bottom.

But, of course, to pay out three times the depth of water demands a large area of swinging room for your boat at the change of tidal flow. In a moderate wind, as the tidal stream slackens, so the boat will tend to swing in a half circle at full scope of the warp until it takes up its new position at the full strength of the opposite tidal stream. This is all very well in an open bay but quite out of the question in the congested harbour or anchorage.

### MOORING A BOAT

It is very often prudent therefore to lay two anchors well apart from each other and to centre the boat between them. This is called mooring your boat. Of course, when doing this, you must make allowance for any rise of tide and the procedure for laying out your first anchor demands that you have more anchor warp available than you are finally going to need when you make it fast inboard. What you have to do, in fact, is to decide the exact point at which you wish your boat to remain: drop your first anchor with slight way on the boat and do not check the boat's way until you have gone an equal distance the other side that first imaginary point. You then drop your second anchor and haul gently in on the first whilst paying out on the second. It sounds a little complicated but it is perfectly easy and when you reckon that you have got the same amount of warp paid out on both anchors, you will be safe in assuming that you are halfway between them. Bearing in mind the state of the tide at the time and allowing for any future rise to High Water you then turn up both anchor warps. With the change of tide therefore, the boat simply ceases to lie to one anchor and commences to lie to the other. See Figure 26.

In the interim period of swing perhaps due to wind, she cannot swing far to either side of an imaginary line on the bottom joining the anchors since simple geometry dictates that two sides of a triangle must be longer than a third side—and we hope your anchor warps are not going to stretch!

This is fine in theory, but you must remember that there are probably twenty other vessels in fairly close proximity who have moored in an identical fashion and I leave you to imagine the possibilities of knitting which could arise if you drop both your anchors across the tops of their anchor warps. Always try to visualise the whereabouts of other boat's anchors by the fashion in which the warps are 'growing' away from their bows.

Even so, despite all precautions, you may find your anchor foul of another boat's and it is seamanlike to carry a small buoy with which the foul anchor can be marked while you weigh your free anchor. You can then go back to your foul anchor which is still on the bottom and try breaking it out by pulling from a

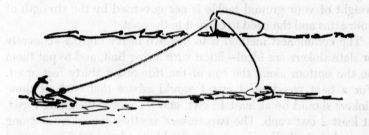

### Figure 26

*A boat moored by two anchors from her bow*

different direction which may well result in your being able to get it to the surface if not actually entangled in a warp, or at least into a position where you can disentangle it. You certainly would not be able to do this if you were still lying to your first anchor. So the buoy comes in very handy.

On occasions it is just not possible to swing at all in a harbour due perhaps to some obstruction or simply congestion of other boats. You may be told to moor bow and stern, in which case the normal procedure described for mooring is followed but one anchor warp is made fast at the bow and one at the stern. This prevents the boat swinging at the change of the tidal stream and obviously it is effected in line with the run of the tide and not across it!

You will be wise to ensure that your boat is orientated bows as near into the wind as possible. If you fail to do this and put her stern up wind, or if perhaps the wind shifts right round, she will be an unhappy creature. Boats, like fish, were built to go forward through the water and are also happier when heading into the wind. To be anchored stern-to-wind will result in any small sea running slopping noisily against her stern and the wind will tend to blow into her cabin through the hatch or under a tent through the flaps, and if it rains, the chances are you will get wet down below.

### PERMANENT MOORINGS

In one's home port, however, it is advisable if the local harbour regulations allow, to lay one's own permanent mooring. Here the weight of your ground tackle is not governed by the strength of your arms and the need to carry it in the boat.

The commonest method is to use two heavy objects—concrete or slate sinkers are ideal—fitted with a ring bolt, and to put them on the bottom along the run of the tide about thirty feet apart. For a boat weighing 4 cwt I would advise that each of these sinkers should be at least 1½ cwt, and for a boat weighing 7 cwt, at least 2 cwt each. The two sinkers are then joined by a strong ground chain (half inch galvanised cable is adequate). This ground chain is shackled securely to the ring bolts on the sinkers and a degree of slackness allowed so that it is not taut. To the centre of this ground chain is then attached a swivel piece, and to this

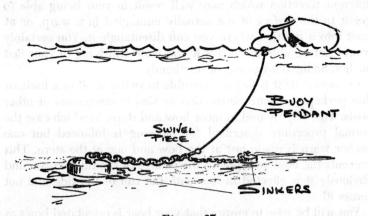

Figure 27
*A Permanent Mooring*

116

No... Please- After YOU Jim...

!

swivel piece a vertical chain (three-eighth inch diameter would be a good size for the average small boat up to 8 cwt). The top of this smaller chain is then shackled to a buoy buoyant enough to carry its weight. This vertical chain is called the buoy pendant and its length should be about twice the depth at High Water at the mooring. The top of the buoy should have a loop attached. A 'bridle'—a stout rope—is led from the bow of your boat through the fairlead, passed through the loop on the buoy and brought back aboard the boat where it is secured. To slip your mooring you simply cast off one end of the bridle and haul it through the buoy loop. See Figure 27.

Frequently harbour authorities have moorings ready laid to save visiting craft the bother of using their own anchors and for the small craft very often a series of vertical buoy pendants are attached to a very long and heavy ground cable. This latter system is sometimes referred to as a trot of moorings. Although in actual fact it is more correctly a line of permanent anchors!

PRAM DINGHIES

While on this subject of moorings, a thought or two on the really small 'tenders' or pram dinghies which are used to get aboard a bigger boat which is anchored on a deep water mooring might be advisable here.

It is very important that these craft should be buoyant when completely swamped, for this 'shore to ship' and vice versa passage can form one of the most hazardous operations on the water. How often does one see a tiny pram, loaded until she has virtually no freeboard with stores and humans, pulling away from a jetty, headed for some boat out in the middle of the harbour? Along goes a thoughtless yacht, and a couple of minutes later her wake puts the whole lot in the drink. Don't overload them: two safe trips are much more worthwhile than one disaster!

One final thought: when the pram is very small, and the two occupants are very large—who gets out first!

# 4

# Safety Afloat

## SAFETY EQUIPMENT

Think of this under two distinct headings: 'UTILITY' and 'CATASTROPHE'. It is surprising how many small craft sailors pride themselves on being fully equipped with gear which comes under the former heading while overlooking the inestimably more important stuff that may only be needed when real catastrophe strikes. Lack of the former can be inconvenient and perhaps uncomfortable. Lack of the latter can cost lives!

Before going afloat anywhere in any boat I always try to visualise beforehand the worst sort of catastrophe taking place in the worst sort of conditions which can arise. This is not gloom and despondency: it's plain common sense.

Much depends of course on the type of water I'm concerned with, but assuming the day's sport is about to take place off an exposed coast, I'll certainly conjure up a vivid impression of the boat completely foundered, her crew in the water, an unexpectedly brisk wind knocking up a choppy sea condition, and all of it taking place dangerously close to a rocky lee shore. It's no use messing about: we might as well be right up against it!

So let us now consider what ought to be included in the equipment of every craft which might conceivably get into that situation.

## 'CATASTROPHE' EQUIPMENT

### 1. Aids to Personal Buoyancy:

A reliable form of buoyancy garment for every member of the crew is a 'must'. In this respect much has been written on the subject of lifejackets and personal buoyancy aids and it is very

119

tempting in a book of this sort to state that a proper lifejacket in the true sense of the word should be worn. To do so would be to avoid facing reality. People just will not wear lifejackets in small dinghies—particularly small sailing dinghies where freedom of movement is essential. On the other hand they will wear a personal buoyancy aid, and they MUST wear it. If you, reader, refuse to wear this: stay ashore. Now what is the difference, and why is there this difference, between a lifejacket and a buoyancy aid?

There are two different requirements here. The function of a lifejacket is to keep a person afloat and adequately supported in such a position that he or she has a good chance of breathing even though severely injured. In fact, an injured person with 35 lbs of buoyancy in a lifejacket tends to get 'dunked' in waves of two feet in height, whether breaking or not, and a swimmer in a personal buoyancy aid is far better off than an inert chap in a full lifejacket.

Certainly a lifejacket should form a part of every seagoing boat's equipment, and in fact any pleasure yacht of forty-five feet and over is required by the Board of Trade Regulations and Recommendations to carry either a Board of Trade approved lifejacket, or a British Standard (B.S.) 3595 lifejacket for every person on board. This does NOT mean that the authorities consider that craft under forty-five feet in length which go to sea need not carry lifejackets. They should, and are strongly recommended to do so. The lifejackets should be in a readily available stowage position in case of emergency and should certainly be donned where risk of being pitched into the water is present. They do suffer the disadvantage when fully inflated of being restrictive to movement and somewhat bulky and it is for this reason that they are not considered suitable for wearing at all times by all personnel afloat.

A personal buoyancy aid is not a lifejacket. It is intended to augment one's natural ability to float when involuntarily immersed for fairly short periods. It is moreover designed to allow swimming by breast stroke or any other stroke for that matter, being less restricting than a lifejacket. If a lifejacket is not being worn a personal buoyancy aid should be worn by all aboard a small craft while afloat. The Ship and Boat Builders National Federation has laid down a set of recommendations governing the minimum requirements in a buoyancy aid, and it is wise to always check before buying that the item does comply with these requirements. Buoyancy aids which do conform are stamped to that effect.

So where are we in our small boat, off an exposed shore, so far as garments that keep you afloat are concerned? It is obvious, is it not? There should be on board a lifejacket for everybody in the boat, and young children and non-swimmers ought to be wearing theirs. The remainder of the crew, if they do not choose to wear the lifejacket available, should wear a personal buoyancy aid.

## 2. Buoyancy in the boat:

It should be quite impossible these days for any small boat to sink completely. If she can she is highly dangerous. I therefore place under the heading of 'catastrophe' equipment either built-in watertight buoyancy tanks which are a part of the boat herself, or really adequate buoyancy bags properly secured to a stout part of the hull or fittings. Whichever it is—and the former is by far the better of the two—MAKE SURE IT WORKS. It is the duty of anyone owning a craft to be quite ruthless about this. If it is a sailing or rowing dinghy fill her with water and capsize her, then sit on her for twenty minutes or so and if there are any leaks at all STOP THEM. This is easy to say: it is not always easy to do. But it is worth doing—at the beginning of every season.

The Class Rules for most sailing dinghies preclude the boat from racing or passing her test for a Measurement Certificate unless this buoyancy of her hull has been properly put to the test, and it is one of the most sensible rules that has come in this day of the small boat boom. Of course, after a certain size it becomes impracticable to swamp a boat: she may have a costly engine aboard, but this is still no reason why the owner should be in any doubt as to whether she will stay afloat if holed or swamped. Tanks can be fitted. Really tough rubber impregnated canvas bags (I suggest those used as boat rollers on beaches) can be inflated and secured beneath thwarts and inside lockers, and this is quite sufficient to keep the boat from going to the bottom provided there are enough of them in relation to the weight of the engine and other non-floating gear.

The boat herself is your first and most worthwhile liferaft if things go wrong, and it's a million times better to be sitting on a semi-submerged liferaft with the confident knowledge that she will remain buoyant, than to be bobbing chin-deep in the water with nothing but a lifejacket or buoyancy aid between you and the kelp. STAY WITH THE BOAT. Unless it is actually taking you into some danger which, by parting from her you can avoid, stay with her. It is the boat the rescue team will be looking for, and it stands a far better chance of being seen than your head in the water!

### 3. *Bailing Equipment:*

More often than not, the sequence in which catastrophe strikes in a small open boat takes the following form. Stimulation: the wind is brisk, the water choppy and it's all very bracing.

Apprehension: the boat is getting a bit of a handful and one doesn't appear to be making such definite way through the water. At this point the safe lee of the nearby headland, or harbour wall, seems suddenly much farther off than you thought in terms of time taken to reach it.

Fear: the boat is beginning to take water over the gunwales, despite all your efforts. This is followed by swamping with that radical change in your attitude towards it all—you're viewing the situation from IN, and no longer ON the water!

The whole thing can be very much prolonged, with the increased chance of the swamping never actually taking place, if a really adequate bailer is ready at hand. I do not mean a bilge pump. A large plastic bucket with stout handle which will not tear off—two buckets for preference—is the answer. It is amazing what a quantity of water can be shovelled out of a boat by an apprehensive crew. By all means, if the boat is suitable, have a self-bailer fitted or a small hand bilge pump, but when the situation is reached where they are beginning to come in 'green'—the bucket is the best thing to take them out 'green'. You will never get a swamped dinghy buoyant again and dry with a hand bilge pump.

### 4. *Distress signals:*

All pyrotechnic distress signals are red in colour with the single exception of smoke signals which are brilliant orange. Signals merely to attract attention, when a craft is not in imminent danger, are white, and large ships sometimes carry a signal to indicate they require a pilot in the form of a blue flare. The latter two are not likely to directly concern us here, but all boats operating in fairly open water ought to carry at least one daylight distress smoke signal, one hand-flare, and two star flare signals. It is not sufficient to carry just one of these star signals for the simple reason that usually the first star signal let off is seen out of the corner of someone's eye ashore or afloat, and merely serves to focus their attention on what is evidently an area where help is needed. It is the second and subsequent star which pinpoints the chap who needs help, and probably guides the rescue craft by a compass bearing if the person or craft in distress cannot actually be seen.

Daylight distress smoke signals specially produced for small boats are available in neat cylinders which can be held in the hand and take up no significant amount of room. They last for three to four minutes and can be used in oil or petrol-covered waters, giving off a dense cloud of smoke.

Hand flares, of around 20,000 candlepower, burning for about one minute, are also produced in small waterproof packs. Their red glow can be seen for several miles in clear daylight and considerably greater distances on a clear night.

Star flare signals which may be held safely in the hand and eject one or more red stars to a good height are really the most likely to attract attention in the first place if any distance off shore, and it is for this reason that I suggest two of these ought to form part of your distress equipment.

The important thing of course is to keep these items completely dry—and do not rely entirely on the plastic waterproof container in which they may be packed for this. It helps, but any small puncture which allows water to penetrate means that it will never evaporate again, and the signal will therefore be subjected to a long insidious soak unless you detect it and remove the plastic cover quickly.

These distress signals are always stamped with the date up to which they are guaranteed to operate, and it is stupid economy to rely on them after such a date.

Remember too that if you are ever in the unhappy position of needing these signals, it is worthwhile, unless your situation is really desperate, to wait until there is some evident chance of their being seen before wildly letting them off. THINK well before igniting them: in such a situation they are very valuable to you, and it is far better to put up with some real discomfort in order to wait the better chance of being seen than to let them off wildly then wish to Heaven you had one left when some vessel passes within visual range—it may even be searching for you!

### 5. *Improvised Liferaft:*

Here, I have in mind some form of improvised liferaft which can, in a real emergency, be perhaps propelled or anchored where it is, while the boat herself may go ashore and be broken up on the rocks. It is that lee shore I am visualising. Take a good look at those rocks and cliff face: if you think you are going to go in there and extract yourself from those foaming great avalanches of water that burst up and over those barnacle-studded nutmeg graters, think again. Somehow you have just got to keep clear of them. If you can stay where you are, time is on your side.

In a really small boat, of course, any form of dinghy or liferaft is out of the question. It is far too bulky to carry and your boat herself is a dinghy anyway. In a twenty foot cruiser certainly you should carry a portable liferaft for such an emergency, but the small boat man is at sea in his liferaft in the first place!

Your best friend here is your anchor. Even though your boat is perhaps completely swamped, if she is drifting into danger through the action of wind or tide, you ought to be able to drop an anchor to keep her where she is. It may be that the swell, which will be getting a much better hold on your swamped boat than it would were she floating normally, will start to drag your anchor. In fact, this is very likely, aided by any tide that is running, for the size of anchor which you are reasonably able to carry in a small boat may not be heavy enough to hold such a pull.

In that case, secure two of those tough canvas inflated boat rollers together, if they form part of your boat's buoyancy equipment. If not, use any items of equipment that have a lot of positive buoyancy. Make yourself fast to these by a length of line and attach that line to the anchor warp near the boat. Then cast the boat adrift: let her go in on the rocks—you will stay where you are with a lot of reserve buoyancy! I'm going to leave you there too. Anyone who gets themselves into that sort of situation frankly deserves to be pulverised: you ought not to be there. That is why I am writing this book. But if you DO ever find yourself in such a pass at least you ought to have the equipment detailed here.

Summarising then the items which ought to come under the heading of 'Catastrophe' equipment:

1. Lifejackets and personal buoyancy aids in the form of garments.
2. Built-in or tied-in buoyancy for the boat.
3. One or two large plastic buckets.
4. Distress signals.
5. Two rubber impregnated buoyancy bags (the best are those used for rolling light dinghies down a beach and are tested to withstand around 500 lbs pressure).
6. Anchor and at least ninety feet of light but tough anchor warp.
7. In addition to this, for use on a small power launch, you should also carry a small fire-extinguisher and a small lifebuoy with about sixty feet of floating line attached, and the name of the boat painted thereon.

'UTILITY' EQUIPMENT

Now for the normal safety equipment which any seaman will automatically carry to work his boat, which comes under the heading of 'Utility' and is extra to the sailing gear and engine.

1. A pair of oars and rowlocks, the latter attached to the craft by a lanyard. Sockets to take the rowlocks. A canoe paddle (or pair of them if there are two of you aboard) is better than nothing, but you will not get far with these in anything of a 'chop' with a brisk wind.
2. A small scoop hand bailer or self-bailer fitted in the hull if a fast-sailing dinghy, or bilge pump discharging into the centreboard casing or overboard if a small power launch.
3. A Bosun's Bag. A stout waterproof canvas bag containing

items such as a screwdriver, pliers, spare shackles, spare seaman's knife and a shackler for undoing jammed shackle pins, a ball of waxed sailmakers twine for whipping ropes ends. You can go on adding to this bosun's bag any special items of chandlery appropriate as spares for your particular boat.

There are some additional items to the above which should be carried if embarking on a coastal cruise, and we will deal with these in Chapter Seven.

### ARTIFICIAL RESPIRATION

The expired air method, commonly known as the 'kiss of life', is now generally taken to be more effective than the external pressure method since it does produce better ventilation of the lungs. It is not perhaps generally recognised that lack of oxygen supply to the brain can cause irreparable harm, if not death, in a very few minutes. For this reason, if you have cause to think that a person in danger of drowning has ceased to breathe, DO NOT DELAY A SECOND. If possible, even while swimming with the drowning person, or perhaps while holding on to a waterlogged boat, a few breaths forced into his lungs will be invaluable. In fact there is an advantage in carrying out the first exchange of breaths while the patient is still in the water, for not only will the water be supporting the patient's body, but his exhalation of the air will be somewhat facilitated by the slight water pressure on his rib cage.

Once ashore the method is as follows, to be carried out with alacrity:

1. Lie the patient on his back, if possible so that his head is slightly higher than his stomach—on a gradual slope will do. While so doing, despatch anyone available for a doctor or trained nurse.

2. Quickly check that the throat and mouth are clear of any obstruction, including the tongue which may be blocking the air passage. Pull it forward.

3. Tilt the patient's head back while gently holding his mouth closed by means of the chin. This tends to stretch the neck a little and ensures a clear airway.

4. Open the patient's mouth, using your hand which is holding his chin to do this. Open your own mouth wide and after taking a good breath in, seal his mouth with yours, and blow, at the same time closing his nostrils either by pinching the nose with your other hand or sealing them both with your cheek. It is important to ensure while carrying out the artificial respiration that his head remains well back. A cushion or rolled towel beneath his shoulders is good for this. If the patient has tightly clenched his mouth, close the lips and cover his nose with your mouth instead, thus applying the air through his nostrils. If it should be that the nose too is blocked, force air through his teeth between his parted lips—it may well be sufficient to inflate his lungs.

5. After exhaling remove your mouth from his and watch for any movement of his chest while you inhale ready for the next blow.

6. If the patient's chest did not rise with your first or second exhalation, check again that his mouth or nose is not blocked, and keeping the head still well tilted back, blow again.

7. It may be that through blowing too hard, air will enter the patient's stomach. If this is observed, turn his head to one side and press gently on his stomach.

8. Start with four quick inflations of the patient's chest to get a build-up of oxygen in his blood, then slow down to from twelve to fifteen inflations per minute—or just blow again each time you see his chest has deflated.

9. While preparing to carry out this mouth-to-mouth artificial respiration breathe deeply through your own open mouth so as to inhale as much oxygen as possible. Remember it is your USED air which is giving him the life-reviving oxygen, so deep breathing first helps. Twenty per cent of air is oxygen. We use about four per cent of this, so there is sufficient remaining in your exhaled breath for the patient, provided his heart is beating and blood circulating.

10. When dealing with small children and babies, a slighter and more rapid rate of inflation should be effected—about twenty per minute—and your own exhalation of air should cease as soon as you feel, or see, the child's chest begin to rise. NEVER BLOW VIOLENTLY INTO A BABY'S lungs; it can cause serious damage.

While effecting the above, get anyone available to remove any tight clothing round the patient's neck or chest, such as a tie, or waistcoat, and try to keep him as warm as possible. Even though there appears to be no response, do not give up. Keep at it until a qualified nurse or doctor arrives. Even though the patient may have revived, it is important that he be despatched to hospital for surveillance as in many cases revival is followed by a relapse which calls for medical equipment.

RULES OF THE ROAD
(International Regulations for Preventing Collision at Sea)

Some small boat operators have unshakeable faith in the policy, 'So long as I keep out of his way there can be no danger of collision.' It's not a bad policy either—far better than that of the chap who thinks, 'I'm bigger than he is, he's sure to alter course soon!'

But remember that in some circumstances avoiding action taken by a craft which has the right of way CAN lead to catastrophe, and it is specifically laid down in the Rules that the vessel having right of way shall maintain her course and speed unless collision is imminent. It is truly astonishing how two craft converging, with nothing else but open water in sight, can end up in a sort of 'love dance' prior to a final desperate swerve which, if luck is on the scene, may result only in loss of paint.

No matter if your craft is small, you should know the rules of the game, and these are available in pamphlet form—about twenty pages of them—from H.M. Stationery Office. It is well worth obtaining a copy.

The extracts which follow are selected as being some of those most necessary to be understood by a small boat handler, and have been condensed and occasionally simplified for easy comprehension. One important point: remember that a sailing craft with her engine running and in gear, regardless of whether she has sail on or not, is considered in the Rules to be a power driven craft. Also a power craft which may be under sail and not propelled by her engine is considered to be a sailing craft.

## STEERING AND SAILING RULES

### POWER MEETING POWER

Rule 18 states that when two power craft are meeting end-on, each alters course to starboard.

Rule 19 states that when two power craft are crossing, so as to risk collision, the boat with the other on her starboard side keeps out of the way.

Note, however, that Rule 25 qualifies this by stating that in a narrow channel a power driven craft of under 65 feet in length shall not hamper the safe passage of a vessel which can navigate only inside such a channel.

### SAIL MEETING SAIL

Rule 17 states that when two sailing craft are approaching one another on opposite tacks the boat on port tack keeps clear, and when two sailing craft are on the same tack the boat to windward must keep clear.

### SAIL MEETING POWER

Rule 20 starts by saying that a power driven vessel must give way to a craft under sail, but immediately qualifies this by saying that a sailing vessel does not have the right to hamper a power driven craft in a narrow channel. In fact an overriding condition which is applicable to all the Rules states that, 'In obeying and construing these Rules due regard shall be had to all dangers of navigation and collision, and any special circumstances, including the limitations of the craft involved, which may render a departure from the above Rules necessary in order to avoid imminent (or immediate) danger.'

Always bear this in mind. It is quite clear: if you happen to be in a fourteen foot sailing dinghy or power launch and a deep-draught yacht is approaching under sail or power in circumstances where you have right of way under the Rules, you must give due regard to his difficulties, and if by sticking to the letter of the law you would be jeopardising his safety in any way, you are under an obligation to keep clear. But take what action you decide on WELL IN ADVANCE. The other craft will be aware that you have right of way and may be about to take avoiding action even at slight risk to himself. If you both take such avoiding action at the same moment—and too late to alter your decision—collision could result.

### OVERTAKING VESSELS

Rule 24 states that notwithstanding anything contained in the Rules every craft overtaking any other shall keep out of the way of the overtaken craft.

Note that to be an overtaking craft you must be closing the other boat from more than two points (22½ degrees) abaft her beam, and no subsequent alteration of the bearing between the two craft shall make the overtaking boat a crossing boat within the meaning of the Rules, or relieve her of the duty of keeping clear of the overtaken boat until she is finally past and clear.

There is an infallible method of ascertaining whether two craft are on a collision course. Take a bearing of the other boat: if it does not alter—you'll hit!

## SOUND SIGNALS FOR CRAFT WITHIN SIGHT OF ONE ANOTHER

Even in a small dayboat, and particularly in a small power driven craft, it is advisable to carry an adequate method of making sound signals, since these are used to indicate a change of course where it is likely to be of concern to another craft. These signals are made on the siren of a large ship or on the foghorn of a small boat. Excellent small gas operated hand foghorns are available from ship's chandlers.

Rule 28 gives the signals:

| | |
|---|---|
| One short blast: | I am directing my course to starboard. |
| Two short blasts: | I am directing my course to port. |
| Three short blasts: | My engines are going astern. |
| | Note that this last signal does not necessarily mean that the craft herself is going astern—she may be still carrying headway with her engines in reverse. |

Five short rapid
blasts:

This is the signal allowed to be made by a craft which considers that another is not taking the appropriate avoiding action thus involving risk of collision.

## SOUND SIGNALS IN POOR VISIBILITY

Rule 15 states that during fog or any other cause of bad visibility a power driven craft of 40 feet or more in length when under way shall make the following signals on her siren or foghorn at intervals of not more than two minutes:

One prolonged blast:     I am making way through the water.
Two prolonged blasts:    I am under way, but stopped.
                               Note that technically a craft is 'under way' so long as she is not attached to the bottom by anchor, moored, aground or berthed alongside.

In similar conditions of low visibility a sailing craft of 40 feet or more in length under way shall make the following signal on her foghorn at intervals of not more than one minute:

One blast:           Craft on starboard tack.
Two blasts:        Craft on port tack.
Three blasts:      Craft with the wind abaft the beam.

All craft over 40 feet in length when at anchor in poor visibility are called upon by the Rules to ring a bell rapidly for five seconds, at intervals of not more than one minute.

A vessel of less than 40 feet in length, and rowing boats, shall not be obliged to give the above mentioned signals, but if she does not she shall make some other efficient sound signal at intervals of not more than one minute.

## VISUAL SIGNALS BY DAY

These take the form of 'shapes' which are hoisted in a prominent position aboard a ship, or adjacent to a coastguard station on land. Rules 4 and 11 lay down the visual signals as follows. (See Figure 28.)

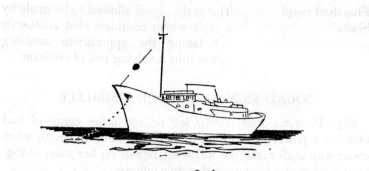

I AM ANCHORED

I AM NOT UNDER COMMAND

I AM AGROUND

*Figure 28*

*Visual Signals on board ship*

*On board ship*

| | |
|---|---|
| One black ball hoisted aloft: | I am at anchor. |
| Two black balls hoisted aloft: | I am not under command. |
| Three black balls hoisted aloft: | I am aground. |

Note that 'not under command' simply means that for some reason or another the craft is manoeuvring with difficulty. Give her a wide berth, but she does not necessarily need assistance.

For craft over 40 feet in length the black balls must be a minimum diameter of two feet. For smaller boats they may be reduced in size.

*Ashore*

| | |
|---|---|
| Black cone, point uppermost: | Gale from Northerly direction imminent. |
| Black cone, point down: | Gale from Southerly direction imminent. |

*Distress*

Rule 31 states that when a craft on the water is in distress and requires assistance, the following shall be used or displayed by her, either together or separately. I quote in full:

(i)   A gun or other explosive signal fired at intervals of about a minute.

(ii)   A continuous sounding with any fog-signal apparatus.

(iii)   Rockets or shells throwing RED stars fired one at a time at short intervals.

(iv)   A signal made by radiotelegraphy or by any other signalling method consisting of the group ········· (SOS) in the Morse Code.

(v)   A signal sent by Radiotelephony consisting of the spoken word 'MAYDAY'. (This is an English version of the French 'm'aidez'—'help me'.)

(vi)   The International Code Signal of distress indicated by N.C.

(vii)   A signal consisting of a square flag having above it or below it a ball, or anything resembling a ball.

(viii)   Flames on the vessel (as from a burning tar barrel, oil barrel, etc.).

(ix)   A rocket parachute flare showing a RED light.

133

(x) A smoke signal giving off a volume of orange coloured smoke.

(xi) Slowly and repeatedly raising and lowering arms outstretched to each side.

## VISUAL SIGNALS BY NIGHT

Lights for craft under way at night are not only intended to indicate their presence, but also the approximate course each is steering relative to the other. It is important therefore that the arcs of visibility of the lights should be accurate. All who go to sea should be familiar with them.

First we will consider the Rules governing power and sailing craft over 65 feet in length.

Rule 2 states that:

POWER CRAFT OVER 150 FEET IN LENGTH shall carry when under way:

| | |
|---|---|
| On the port side: | a red light shining from straight ahead to two points (22½ degrees) abaft the beam, visible for a minimum of 2 miles. |
| On the starboard side: | a green light shining from straight ahead to two points (22½ degrees) abaft the beam, visible for a minimum of 2 miles. |
| At the foremast: (or forepart of craft) | a white light shining through an arc ahead of the craft from two points abaft the beam on one side to two points abaft the beam on the other. This light shines therefore through an unbroken arc of 225 degrees. It must be vertically above the keel and not less than 20 feet in height above the uppermost continuous deck. |
| Abaft the above white light: | a second white light shining through a similar arc, but at least 15 feet higher than the other and in the horizontal plane it must be at least three times the vertical distance away. |

POWER CRAFT UNDER 150 FEET IN LENGTH when under way shall carry the same lights as power craft over 150 feet in length but the second masthead white light is optional.

At the stern:

Rule 10, which is applicable to all craft, states that they shall carry at the stern a white light shining across an arc at the stern of the craft from two points (22½ degrees) abaft the beam on one side to two points abaft the beam on the other side. This light therefore shines through an arc of 135 degrees—67½ degrees on either side. It completes that section of a circle which is left unlit by the port and starboard lights, and must be visible for at least 2 miles.

## A SAILING CRAFT UNDER WAY

Rule 5 states that a sailing vessel under way shall carry port, starboard and stern lights of the same colour and characteristics as a power craft except that she does not carry either of the white masthead lights. She may however—at the moment it is optional —carry at her masthead one red light above one green light, separated so as to be clearly distinguished, and visible over an arc of the horizon similar to the white masthead lights of a power craft. They must be visible for a distance of at least 2 miles.

## VESSELS AT ANCHOR

Rule 11 states that any vessel—power or sail—when anchored is required to carry an anchor light as follows:

Craft under 150 feet in length: at the forepart a white light visible all round the horizon at a distance of at least two miles.

Craft over 150 feet in length: one light as described above, and in addition at or near the stern and not less than 15 feet lower than the forward light, another such light. Both lights to be visible for a minimum distance of 3 miles.

So much for the bigger boats. But the authorities have recognised that it is not always practicable to carry the signals detailed above in really small boats and have therefore made provision as follows:

Rule 7 states: 'Power-driven vessels of less than 65 feet in length, vessels under oars or sails of less than 40 feet in length, and rowing boats, when under way shall not be required to carry the lights mentioned in Rule 2, 3 (not quoted above—it applies to vessels towing) and 5, but if they do not carry them they shall be provided with the following lights:'

I extract in abbreviated form:

POWER CRAFT UNDER 65 FEET IN LENGTH

(a) (i) Forward at a height of not less than 9 feet above the gunwale, a white light visible at least 3 miles and covering an arc as detailed for the masthead lights in Rule 2.

(a) (ii) Port and starboard sidelights as detailed in Rule 2, to be carried not less than 3 feet below the white light detailed in (i) above and visible at least one mile. These port and starboard lights may however be housed in a combined lantern provided the arcs of visibility remain unaltered, and provided the lantern is secured to the boat not less than 3 feet below the white light.

POWER CRAFT UNDER 40 FEET IN LENGTH

(c) May carry the white light in (a) (i) above at a less height than 9 feet above the gunwale, but it must not be less than 3 feet above the sidelights or combined lantern detailed in (a) (ii).

The stern light detailed in Rule 10 is advised, but the qualification is made that if for any good reason it is not possible to fix this stern light, an electric torch or lighted lantern shall be kept at hand ready for immediate use, and shall on the approach of an overtaking vessel be shown in time to prevent risk of collision.

SAILING CRAFT, OR CRAFT UNDER OARS OF LESS THAN 40 FEET IN LENGTH

I quote the rule in full:

(d) Except as in (f) below the above craft 'shall, if they do not carry the sidelights, carry, where it can best be seen a lantern showing a green light on one side and a red light on the other, of such a character as to be visible at a distance of at least one mile, and so fixed that the green light shall not be seen on the port side, nor the red light on the starboard side. Where it is not possible to fix this light it shall be kept ready for immediate use and shall be exhibited in sufficient time to prevent collision and so that the green light shall not be seen on the port side nor the red light on the starboard.'

## SMALL ROWING BOATS

(f) 'Whether under oars or sail shall only be required to have ready at hand an electric torch or a lighted lantern showing a white light which shall be exhibited in sufficient time to prevent collision.'

. . .

So you see in all types of craft the Rules are sensible and there is appreciation of the difficulties of really small boats. Even so, the collision regulations are as valid for a dinghy as they are for the larger craft, and it is very necessary that the day and night signals applying to both are properly understood.

## BUOYAGE SYSTEM

By international agreement—pleasant thought!—the shapes, colours and light characteristics (if any) of buoys have been broadly standardised, although some harbours may impose their own local buoyage systems which differ from the main principle in various respects.

Unless one has detailed local knowledge of the waters it is wise to adhere to the channels indicated by the buoys even in a small craft.

The international system which concerns us here in the coastal waters of the United Kingdom is known as the Uniform Buoyage System and before one can start talking with any meaning in terms of 'this side' or 'that side' or any direction for that matter, one has to have a reference point to which such instructions may be related. Since we are dealing here with direction it is reasonable to relate any instructions to some unambiguous direction which all can understand and ascertain.

The reference chosen is that direction in which the main flood tidal stream flows. Everything in the Uniform System of Buoyage relates to that, and the direction of flow of the main flood tidal stream is shown in Figure 7. What is more, it will be quite evident that this flood stream must always flow INTO estuaries and harbours. The ebb stream will flow OUT of them.

137

Having established that, it is necessary to clearly define what is meant by 'starboard hand' and 'port hand' since these are the terms used to describe channel buoys which indicate the limits of safe navigable depth in a channel.

Starboard Hand Buoy:   This is a buoy which must be left on the right hand side of a mariner when entering an estuary, river or harbour from seaward—that is when proceeding WITH the main flood stream of tide.

                                       The assumption is, of course, that the mariner is looking in the direction he's heading!

Port Hand Buoy:   This is a buoy which must be left on the left hand side of a mariner in similar circumstances.

It will be obvious that the buoys must, when going OUT of harbour, etc. (against the main flood stream) be left on the opposite side.

Occasionally, when there is a shoal or some other large obstruction in the middle of a wide channel, on either side of which a craft may pass, a buoy is placed in such a position that the boat, having chosen the channel required, has plenty of time to alter course into the chosen channel. Frequently one channel is deeper and wider than the other, in which case this is referred to as the main channel. So we have need for a third type of buoy.

Middle Ground Buoy:   This is a buoy that may be left on either hand of the mariner when proceeding with the main flood stream.

This middle ground buoy requires a little further explanation. It will be evident that where the estuary for instance is long and wide, such as the entrance to the Thames, these 'middle grounds' or shoals can be extensive. In such a case one middle ground buoy would be placed at the seaward end and another at its inshore end. To distinguish the one from the other a 'topmark' is fixed to each as shown in Figure 29.

Sometimes when entering an estuary or harbour from seaward

the channel may divide into two separate channels which do not again join. In such a case only the seaward middle ground buoy would be required.

It is necessary to be able to distinguish without any doubt at the greatest possible distance the type of channel buoy one is approaching. The shapes and colours therefore must be arranged to eliminate confusion as far as possible. They are illustrated in Figure 29 and described below:

Starboard Hand Buoy:   *Shape*: Conical.
                                  *Colour*: Black, or black and white chequers.
                                  *Light* (if any): White, showing 1, 3 or 5 flashes (an odd number).

Port Hand Buoy:   *Shape*: Can.
                                  *Colour*: Red, or red and white chequers.
                                  *Light* (if any): Red, showing any number of flashes up to four. OR white, showing 2, 4 or 6 flashes (an even number).

Middle Ground Buoy:   *Shape*: Spherical.
                                  *Colour*: Red and white horizontal bands where the main channel is to starboard. Black and white horizontal bands where main channel is to port. Red and white horizontal bands where channels of equal importance.

Topmarks on middle ground buoys:

Main channel to right:   Outer end—a red can.
                                  Inner end—a red 'T'.

Main channel to left:   Outer end—a black cone.
                                  Inner end—a black diamond.

Channels of equal importance:   Outer end—a red sphere.
                                  Inner end—a red St George's Cross.

In addition to these main channel buoys there are other navigation buoys which under the Uniform System of Buoyage follow a prescribed shape and colour, for instance:

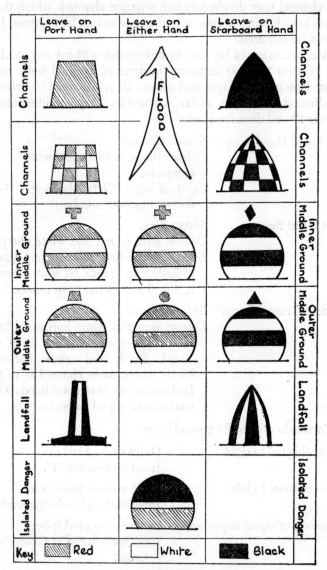

*Figure 29*
The Uniform System of Buoyage

*Landfall buoys* are positioned off shore to help a craft establish her exact position so that a correct approach to a channel from seaward may be made. These follow the shapes laid down for channel buoys and are coloured in black and white or red and white vertical stripes. If lit they have a light of some flashing character.

*Isolated danger buoys* are used to mark isolated shoals or rocks surrounded by deep water. They are spherical in shape and coloured with wide black and red horizontal bands separated by a narrow white band. If lit, the light will be white or red of some flashing character.

*Mid channel buoys* sometimes mark the middle of a wide channel, the banks of which are marked by the port and starboard hand buoys. They have the advantage of effectively separating the two lanes of incoming and outgoing craft. Their shape is distinctive and can be almost anything so long as it differs largely from the main channel buoy shapes. Their colours may be black and white or red and white vertical stripes, and the light, if any, will be distinctively different from nearby lights on buoys at the sides of the channel.

*Wreck marking buoys.* As well as marking the wreck, these follow the shapes laid down for channel buoys to further indicate to a craft the hand on which the buoy should be left. They are always coloured green, with the word 'wreck' painted in white on the side. If lit, a starboard hand wreck buoy will show a triple green flash every 10 or 15 seconds. A port hand wreck buoy shows a double green flash every 10 seconds, while a wreck buoy which may be left on either hand shows a single green flash every 5 seconds, or very rapid green flashes for 7 seconds, followed by 3 seconds without light, then the next series of rapid flashes for 7 seconds.

When taking a power craft through a navigable channel always keep to the starboard hand of the channel whether entering or leaving. Just remember this rule to be opposite that of a vehicle on the road.

Channel buoys marked on charts are drawn with the shapes described and if lit have a small purple blob against them with the characteristic of the light printed in abbreviated form alongside.

# 5

# Aids to Seamanship

CORDAGE

You will come across ropes made from three basically different materials today: natural vegetable fibres, synthetic fibres and wire.

NATURAL FIBRES

There are four main types in use; Manila, Hemp, Sisal and Coir, and from consideration of strength they may be grouped in that order, Manila being the strongest although a top quality Italian Hemp can be stronger than some Manilas.

Manila rope is made from fibres in the leaf sheath of the abaca plant which grows chiefly in the Phillipine Islands, being shipped from the port of Manila (whence the name). It is gold-brown in colour when new, flexible and strong, with good resistance to chafe and weathering.

Hemp rope is made from fibres of the hemp plant stem which grows in many parts of the world, though the best quality for ropemaking purposes is acknowledged as coming from Italy. It is pale grey in colour, tends to be more flexible than Manila and apart from the top quality Italian brands is generally not quite so strong as Manila.

Sisal rope is made from leaves of a member of the cactus family called Agave sisalana which grows in Kenya, Tanzania, Haiti and Java. Less flexible than either Hemp or Manila it is the colour of pale straw and not so strong as either of the former. It is also less resistant to chafe and weathering.

Coir rope is made from fibre in the husk of Ceylonese coconuts and is very hairy and brown in colour. It is about one fifth as strong as Manila rope of equal size and half the weight, but it has the advantage of floating in water. It does not weather well, and soon succumbs to chafe. It also rots quickly if stowed away wet.

## CONSTRUCTION OF NATURAL FIBRE ROPES

Whatever the material chosen for making up a natural fibre rope the first process is to comb out the leaf, husk or stem into its component fibres. Generally these are between two and four feet in length and are then stroked out so that they overlap each other to form a long even ribbon. This is then carefully twisted to bind the fibres firmly together by friction into a long continuous 'yarn'. A number of these yarns—perhaps seven or nine or more depending on the required size of the finished rope—are then twisted together to form 'strands'.

These strands are usually made about 150 fathoms in length, and as in the process of making up the yarns, the twist which is given to them may be either left handed or right handed. Three, or sometimes four of the strands are now 'laid up' into a rope by twisting them together and at the same time rotating the individual strands in the same direction as the twist. This prevents the yarns of which the strands are made from themselves untwisting as the strand is laid-up.

As you may imagine this laying-up of the strands into a rope results in the finished rope being somewhat shorter in length than the original strands since these are, as it were, spiralling within the rope. In fact, the 150 fathom strand will make up a rope about 120 fathoms in length, and this is the length of a full coil of rope.

So you have four stages: fibres, yarns, strands and rope, and if a rope is laid-up from three strands (which is by far the most common way) it is said to be hawser-laid.

## MEASUREMENT AND STRENGTH OF ROPES

All ropes and wire have since the early days of sail been measured by their circumference. This is roughly three times the diameter. There is a tendency today, however, particularly in commercial fields, to give the size of ropes by their diameter, so it is best always to query or specify which method of measurement is being used.

A rough and ready method of determining the breaking strain and safe working load of manila, hemp and sisal is to square the circumference in inches and divide by three to give the breaking strain in tons. The safe working load is then approximately one-sixth of this breaking strain.

SYNTHETIC ROPES

There are four main types of these chemically manufactured ropes on the market today, namely Nylon, Terylene, Polypropylene and Polyethylene. The latter two are very light and will float in water.

Synthetic rope construction differs from that of natural fibres in that the component yarns, instead of being made up of short lengths of fibre, are of one continuous length. They are twisted into strands and laid up into ropes in much the same manner as the natural cordage but the resultant rope has some qualities which are lacking in natural fibre cordage. They are for instance virtually unaffected by oils and immune from attack by mould, bacteria and insects.

In addition to the three-strand hawser-laid synthetic ropes, a very flexible multi-plait terylene rope is frequently used today for the sheets of small sailing craft. This has the great advantage that it will not kink—a habit of all hawser-laid ropes unless handled with care.

Tables of recommended construction for synthetic ropes when used as sheets, halyards, anchor and mooring warps together with the recommended sizes for overall lengths and tonnage of craft are published by the leading rope manufacturers and are available from most ship's chandlers who sell cordage.

Plate 5 shows the construction of three types of synthetic ropes and one wire, such as are frequently used in small craft today together with their minimum strengths.

When used within its safe working load, terylene will stretch about fifteen per cent of its length and has good powers of recovery after such stretching. It is also virtually unaffected by extremely low temperatures, but where excessive heat is caused (at 260 degrees Centigrade and above) it will start melting. This can show itself in the rope by a glazed look where the material has fused at the point where heat has been generated. This can occur where excessive friction takes place, and does of course affect the strength of the rope. Any area so affected should be cut out of the rope's length.

Nylon and terylene ropes are almost always silver-white in colour. The polypropylene and polyethylene floating ropes are generally dyed a brilliant yellow, orange, blue or green. Tests and usage have suggested that certain of these latter two types of man-made rope, while being adequate for tasks where a constant straight pull is exerted, have snapped without warning at chafe points such as fairleads and cleats where a jerking strain is applied. The continued action of a boat moored or anchored or at a berth in choppy water might cause this. It would appear that in addition to actual fusing due to heat generation there also takes place a form of material fatigue possibly due to molecular disturbance which can result in a sudden separation.

Nylon and terylene ropes are respectively about three times and twice the strength of the same size natural fibre ropes.

## WIRE ROPE

As in synthetic hawser-laid rope, a wire rope is made up of many small wires which are continuous throughout its entire length. In the larger size wire ropes these small wires are twisted into strands and the strands laid up into the finished rope. Most wire ropes consist of six strands, the separate wires of which are twisted around a jute or wire core which runs right through the centre of each strand. The strands are then laid up around a hemp or jute heart which acts as a cushion into which the strands bed when bent or under strain, and this heart also has the function of absorbing the linseed oil with which the rope should be periodically wiped, so that under strain when the heart is squeezed, the oil is pushed out between the strands. It thus both protects from rust and lessens the friction by lubrication.

There are, however, many different constructions of wire rope for a wide variety of specific jobs. You will usually find that the standing rigging such as forestay and shrouds of smaller sailing craft and dinghies are of ⅜ inch circumference stainless steel wire made up of twelve single strands wrapped around a heart of seven single strands, as illustrated in Plate 5. This is known as 1x19 construction, since each strand is a single wire and there are nineteen of them. This size and construction of stainless steel wire has a minimum breaking strain of 1680 lbs.

## KNOTS AND SPLICES

The great thing about learning to tie knots is to tie them— again and again and interminably again. If you imagine, when after five minutes with a mangled piece of rope you have persuaded it into the contortions shown in the photographs here, that you have learned to tie a knot—think again! Try it next week without the photo and see what happens.

No: you've just got to live with a rope, use it if you can, get your nearest and dearest to participate constantly (you'll soon find out if it's mutual) and after a long long time, when all of them just fall happily into place in your expert hands THEN, and only then, provided you constantly practise, you can truly say: 'I have mastered knots!'

You are now halfway on the road to success. The other half is completed when you can also say, 'and I know when and how to use them.' It's not a bit of use putting a clove hitch round your neck when you're just about to be hoisted thirty feet on to the deck of a tanker. How and when to use knots is just as important as knowing how to tie them.

The test of a reliable knot is whether it will hold under any strain and yet be easily and quickly untied when the strain is removed. On occasions it is also desirable for a knot to be quickly 'slipped' when the strain is still on the rope.

For this reason I have included alongside three of the knots illustrated in the photographs an example of the same knot incorporating a slip. The important thing to remember when making a quick-release slipknot is to leave enough of the rope end free to get a firm grip, because when a full strain is on the rope it sometimes takes a fair pull to snatch the slip 'bight' free and release the whole knot. Equally important of course is the need to have enough of the slip 'bight' rove, so that there is no chance of it slipping free accidentally while under strain.

First let us define the terms used when making knots so that we can talk about them with accuracy. See Figure 30.

146

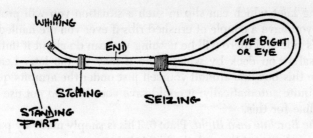

WHIPPING

END

THE BIGHT OR EYE

STOPPING

SEIZING

STANDING PART

*Figure 30*

*Terms used when making knots*

*The bare end* is the actual end of a rope where it has been cut to give a required length. Such a bare end should always be treated with a whipping.

*Whipping* is a tight binding of thin cord for about half an inch or so, to prevent the strands of the rope from unlaying.

*The tail end* is that length at either end of a rope which is used to make either a knot or an eye or bight.

*An eye or bight* is a loop in a rope. To make an eye or bight is to form a loop.

*The standing part* is that part of the rope which is near to the eye or knot.

*Seizing* is a strong binding applied with small stout cord round two ropes (or two parts of the same rope) which will prevent them moving in relation to each other. The verb is 'to seize'.

*Stopping* is a temporary fastening applied with a light cord to hold a bare end of a rope in place—perhaps to the standing part of the rope—in order that it cannot 'work back' after the rope has been in constant use, which might result in a knot becoming loosened. Unlike a seizing it is not intended to carry any strain.

Now let us take a look at some useful knots and see when and how they are used.

*The Bowline and bowline with slip.* Plate 6. This is a most useful knot forming a bight of any required size in the end of a rope. Unlike a noose, this bight cannot slip and become smaller, and for this reason one should use a bowline to make a line fast around oneself if about to be pulled out of the water, or as a lifeline should there be risk of falling into the water. If you use a

147

wrong knot which can slip in such a situation you will probably find you have a couple of crushed ribs if ever you are hauled up a ship's side and there will be nothing you can do about it until you are safely on deck by which time it may be too late. Learn to make this bowline around yourself just under the armpits quickly and quite automatically: it could save your life. Do not use a slip bowline for this.

*The Bowline on a Bight.* Plate 6. This is simply made by passing the standing part through the bight. It is a noose.

*The Fisherman's Bend.* Plate 6. This is splendid for securing a rope's end to a ringbolt or post on a jetty, or to the ring of an anchor. In the latter case the end should be stopped back to the standing part.

*The Sheet Bend and Sheet Bend with Slip.* Plate 7. This is used for joining two ropes of unequal thickness. The first bight is formed in the thicker of the two ropes and the thin rope worked round it as shown.

*The Reef Knot and 'Granny'.* Plate 7. The reef knot is for joining two ropes of equal thickness. This should never be used in place of a sheet bend if the ropes are of unequal thickness. Be very careful when making a reef knot to cross the ends opposite ways each time they are 'knotted'—i.e. pass the ends left over right and then right over left, otherwise you will make a 'granny' as illustrated to the right in the photograph. The granny is no knot, for it will slip and pull out.

*The Rolling Hitch.* Plate 7. This is used for securing a rope to a spar, or another much larger rope where the eventual pull is to be in one direction only. It is made by passing the end twice round the spar or rope, taking each turn across the standing part and finishing with a separate half hitch round the spar. Always make the first two turns at that end from which the pull is to be applied.

*The Clove Hitch.* Plate 8. This is very often used to secure a rope to a rail or post because it is a very satisfying sort of knot to make. People who are not naturally 'knotters' become hypnotised by their inability to master its simplicity and you will always find it included in every book on knots. I cannot think why. Here it is again, and I'm presenting it too, but to my mind it has two major faults: if the post or spar to which it is attached is free to rotate, it will do so when the strain is applied because the pull comes from the extremity of the radius of the spar. When the spar rotates the clove hitch will happily unroll until the rope comes free. Secondly, if the strain is applied from a direction more or less in line with the spar, the clove hitch can easily slip along. So remember, a clove hitch is fine so long as the spar to which it is attached is very rigid and the direction of pull on the rope is to be nearly at right angles to the post.

*The Timber Hitch.* Plate 8. This is a good knot for securing a rope's end to a spar or bale provided it matters not that the item is subjected to a squeezing strain, for the timber hitch forms a noose. It suffers the disadvantage that when the rope is allowed to slacken the timber hitch can easily untie itself and fall free. It is often used in conjunction with a simple half hitch for hoisting or towing spars where the strain is constant. If the spar is thicker at one end, the half hitch (from which the pull is directly exerted) should always be at the thick end with the timber hitch slightly farther down the spar toward the thinner end. This eliminates any possibility of either hitch pulling off the end.

*The Quick Release Hitch on cleat.* Plate 8. When belaying a rope to a cleat, it is never advisable to finish off with a 'jamming turn' by crossing the rope back under its own part. Under strain, or when swelling takes place after wetting natural fibre rope, it can be very difficult to cast off. Sometimes however it may be felt that the turns alone around the cleat or belaying pin might jump off unless prevented, and in this case the slip hitch illustrated is useful, since a hard jerk on the free end will always free the bight so that the rope can be cast off quickly.

*The Figure-of-eight.* Plate 8. This is a stopper knot, used to prevent the end of a sheet unreeving through a sheetlead. It cannot jam, no matter how tight it is pulled.

*The Eyesplice.* Plate 9. This makes a permanent eye in the end of a three or more stranded rope. A braided, multiplait rope cannot be spliced in this fashion.

Before starting it is best to put a whipping on the rope at about a distance of six times the circumference of the rope from the end. Unlay the rope back to this whipping, and put a whipping on the end of each strand at its bare end. If you do not do this the strands will start to unlay, making it very difficult to persuade them neatly through the opened lays of the rope as you proceed. On smaller ropes as illustrated this is not necessary.

Form an eye of the size required, and hold the whipping which is preventing the whole rope unlaying against the standing part so that the eye is to your left and the unlaid strands of the rope toward your right. Place one of the three strands on top and allow the other two to fall, one either side the rope down out of the way. The lay immediately beneath the single strand on top is now prised open and this strand is passed from you, through the hole, and out at the far side away from you, being pulled neatly down into the rope and twisted as it is pulled to prevent its component fibres becoming loose.

Give the rope and eye a half twist so that one of the remaining two strands is on top. Now open up the lay immediately beneath it and pass this strand in exactly the same manner through the hole so formed—that is away from you, pulling it neatly taut from the far side.

There is only the last strand now to deal with, and this is the trickiest. Take a look at the 'tucks' you have just completed: you will see that there is only one gap between the strands at their level which has not got a strand emerging from it. It is from out of there that the third strand must come, but again I emphasise it has to be FROM you through the hole made by opening up the lay of the rope and out of this gap on the far side. This completes the first tuck, and if you have done it correctly, all three strands will be emerging about 120 degrees apart from each other at the same level.

From now on it is simple: each strand continues to go over the one beneath it and under the one next to it. When splicing natural fibre ropes such as manila, hemp or sisal, a minimum of three tucks is necessary, but with terylene and nylon ropes where there is very much less friction between the strands, at least five tucks should be made before cutting off the ends. These may either then be whipped, or stranded out and a 'serving' bound neatly over them. This word 'serving' is really another term for whipping, but it is used when the whipping is for the purpose of concealing rather than actually holding together.

*The Common Whipping.* As we have already seen, a whipping is for preventing the end of a rope unlaying when it is cut, and there are various methods of doing this, all referred to as whippings, such as West Country whipping, sailmakers whipping and American whipping. The one described here, if made tightly and properly, is perfectly adequate.

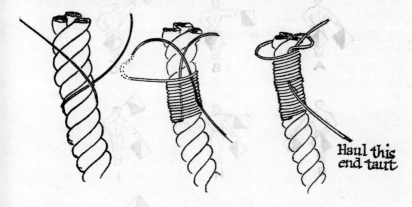

Haul this
end taut

*Figure 31*

*The Common Whipping*

Place the end of the whipping twine along the end of the rope as shown in Figure 31 and pass the turns of twine tightly round the rope trapping the end firmly beneath the turns. Turn the twine against the lay of the rope and work towards the rope's end. After about a quarter of an inch of whipping lay the other end of the twine along the rope and pass the remaining turns over it taking the loop of twine over the end of the rope with each turn. When you have run out of loop, pull this second end of the twine through the turns you have passed over it until taut, which completes the last turn round the rope. Cut off both loose ends.

SEMAPHORE

Comparatively few people are able to send, and even fewer to receive messages, by this method of signalling. It is a pity, for it is a valuable method of communication over short distances, and I often wonder why it is not included in the curriculum of all schools: it would be great fun for the kids, and of much use later

# Semaphore

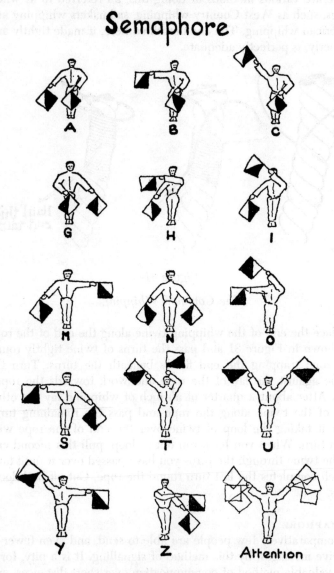

**Figure 32**

Semaphore

# Semaphore

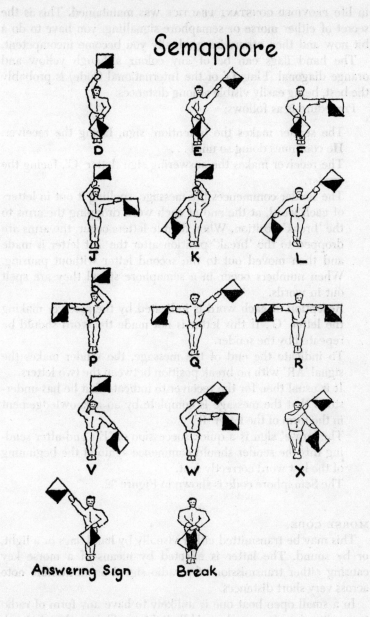

Answering Sign        Break

153

in life PROVIDED CONSTANT PRACTICE was maintained. This is the secret of either morse or semaphore signalling: you have to do a bit now and then otherwise gradually you become incompetent.

The hand flags can be of any colour although yellow and orange diagonal (Flag 'O' of the International Code) is probably the best, being easily visible at long distances.

Procedure is as follows:

> The sender makes the 'attention' sign, facing the receiver. He continues doing so until . . .
> The receiver makes the answering sign (letter 'C', facing the sender.
> The sender commences the message, spelling it out in letters of each word, at the end of each word dropping the arms to the 'break' position. When double letters occur, the arms are dropped to the 'break' position after the first letter is made and then moved out to the second letter without pausing. When numbers occur in a semaphore signal they are spelt out in words.
> Reception of each word is indicated by the receiver making the letter 'C'. If this letter is not made the word should be repeated by the sender.
> To indicate the end of the message, the sender makes the signal 'AR' with no break position between the two letters.
> It is usual then for the receiver to indicate that he has understood that the message is complete by an acknowledgement in the form of the letter 'R'.
> The 'erase' sign is a quick succession of 'E's and after sending this the sender should commence again at the beginning of the last word correctly sent.
> The Semaphore code is shown in Figure 32.

MORSE CODE

This may be transmitted either visually by hand flags or a light, or by sound. The latter is effected by means of a morse key causing either transmission of a radio signal or an audible note across very short distances.

In a small open boat one is unlikely to have any form of radio transmitter/receiver, and an Aldis light or efficient electric torch is probably the most frequently used method of sending morse signals. Hand flags (or even just the arms) however can be used, and the method is shown in Figure 33.

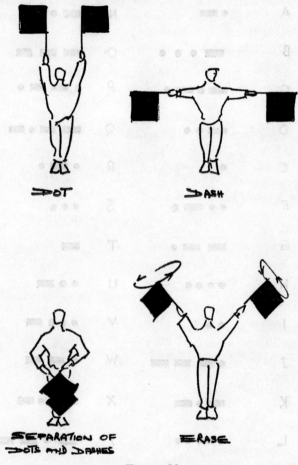

DOT

DASH

SEPARATION OF DOTS AND DASHES

ERASE

*Figure 33*
*Sending Morse Code by hand flags*

Whatever the method used, the procedure is as follows:

The sender makes the call signal 'AA' 'AA' 'AA'.

The receiver sends the answering signal 'T'.

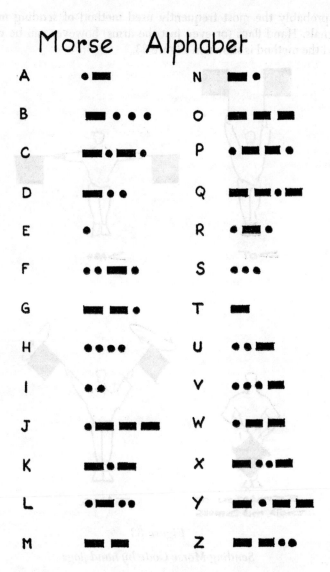

# Morse   Alphabet

| | | | |
|---|---|---|---|
| A | • ▬ | N | ▬ • |
| B | ▬ • • • | O | ▬ ▬ ▬ |
| C | ▬ • ▬ • | P | • ▬ ▬ • |
| D | ▬ • • | Q | ▬ ▬ • ▬ |
| E | • | R | • ▬ • |
| F | • • ▬ • | S | • • • |
| G | ▬ ▬ • | T | ▬ |
| H | • • • • | U | • • ▬ |
| I | • • | V | • • • ▬ |
| J | • ▬ ▬ ▬ | W | • ▬ ▬ |
| K | ▬ • ▬ | X | ▬ • • ▬ |
| L | • ▬ • • | Y | ▬ • ▬ ▬ |
| M | ▬ ▬ | Z | ▬ ▬ • • |

*Figure 34*

*The Morse Alphabet*

156

The sender indicates the end of the message by transmitting the letters 'AR'.

It is usual for the receiver to indicate that he has understood that the message is complete by an acknowledgement in the form of the letter 'R'.

If using hand flags, normally both arms should be used, but if this is difficult or perhaps impossible one arm can be used.

Figures 34 and 35 show the Morse alphabet and the Morse numerals.

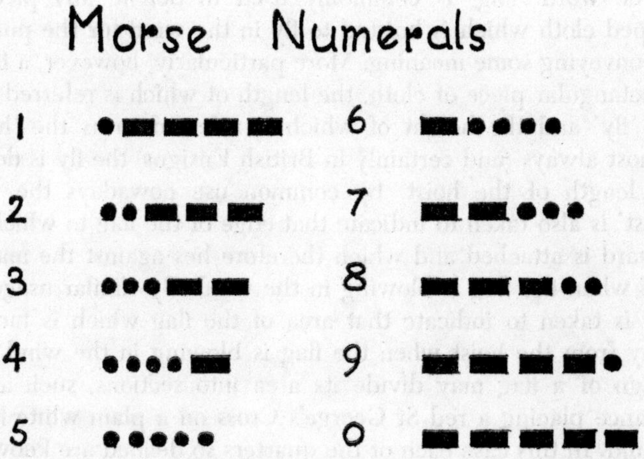

## Morse Numerals

| | | | |
|---|---|---|---|
| 1 | ●▬▬▬▬ | 6 | ▬●●●● |
| 2 | ●●▬▬▬ | 7 | ▬▬●●● |
| 3 | ●●●▬▬ | 8 | ▬▬▬●● |
| 4 | ●●●●▬ | 9 | ▬▬▬▬● |
| 5 | ●●●●● | 0 | ▬▬▬▬▬ |

*Figure 35*

*The Morse Numerals*

Communication between two craft in morse by means of sound signals is quite possible (though it tends to be very slow) but is not really to be recommended, since some of the morse symbols coincide with signals used in the Regulations for Prevention of Collision at Sea, and could easily lead to confusion—certainly this sound method should not be used in a busy fairway.

FLAGS AND THEIR USAGE

Wherever yachts are operating you will observe them to be wearing a few different types of ensigns and flying a wide variety of flags. A chap in a small dayboat may consider this to be some-what academic and unlikely ever to be applicable to him. But he will certainly be at a distinct disadvantage—and perhaps on occasions be made to feel rather a fool—if such ensigns and flags hold no significance for him whatever.

Let us scan briefly the whole gamut of coloured cloths we sailors are given to hoisting, not without justifiable pride, in the rigging and other parts of our craft.

DEFINITIONS

The word 'flag' is commonly used to denote any piece of shaped cloth which is hoisted to fly in the wind for the purpose of conveying some meaning. More particularly, however, a flag is a rectangular piece of cloth, the length of which is referred to as the 'fly' and the height of which is referred to as the 'hoist'. Almost always (and certainly in British Ensigns) the fly is double the length of the hoist. By common use nowadays the word 'hoist' is also taken to indicate that edge of the flag to which the halyard is attached and which therefore lies against the mast or staff when the flag is blowing in the wind. By similar usage the 'fly' is taken to indicate that area of the flag which is farthest away from the hoist when the flag is blowing in the wind. The design of a flag may divide its area into sections, such as for instance placing a red St George's Cross on a plain white back-ground. In this case each of the quarters so defined are known as 'cantons', an upper and lower canton at the hoist and similarly at the fly.

A burgee is a triangular piece of cloth the hoist of which, other than in a few exceptional cases, is two-thirds the length of the fly.

A pendant (or pennant) is a rectangular piece of cloth from out of which, at the fly, has been cut a wide 'V' leaving two points. Such a shape is called 'swallow-tailed'. Generally, but not always, the total length is double that of the hoist.

Flags, burgees and pendants are coloured and bear designs which have definite meanings, not only within the International Code of Signals which incorporates forty different flags, but also when used at sea to indicate the nationality of a craft, the pres-ence of Royalty, the status or office of a boat's owner within his yacht club, and in the merchant service the name of the line owning the ship. Generally, people speak of wearing an ensign and flying everything else.

ENSIGNS

Commonly known as 'the colours', an ensign is the national flag and indicates the nationality of the owner of a craft. The British use five types of ensigns, and they rank as follows in order of seniority:

> The White Ensign
> The Blue Ensign
> The Blue Ensign defaced
> The Red Ensign defaced
> The Red Ensign

All of the above, with the exception of the last, are known as Special Ensigns and their use is governed by very strict regulations.

Privilege to wear a special ensign is granted by the Secretary of State for Defence to certain yacht clubs which are listed in the Navy List. Owners of yachts seen to be wearing a special ensign will have made application through their yacht club, and the British Ensign Warrant to wear such special ensign will have been issued to the yacht only on condition that the owner of the yacht is a member of such a privileged club. Moreover, the Warrant is issued to the yacht, and not to the yacht owner, being in fact the national colours of the yacht.

An owner has no right to wear a special ensign other than on board his yacht to which the Warrant has been issued, and the ensign should never be worn without the burgee of the privileged yacht club being flown at the same time.

Normally an ensign is worn at the stern of a vessel, hoisted on its own flagstaff. If, however, this is impracticable—perhaps for reasons of rough weather, or in the case of H.M. Ships, when 'cleared for action' in wartime—it may be worn from the peak of the gaff on the mainmast. In peacetime H.M. Ships wear an ensign at sea when in sight of land or other ships. Ships in harbour hoist their ensigns at 0800 between 25th March and 20th September, lowering them at sunset, and from 21st September to 24th March they are hoisted at 0900 and lowered at sunset or 2100 whichever is the earlier.

It is good manners for yachts entitled to wear ensigns to synchronise their time for hoisting or lowering them with that of any H.M. Ship which may be in harbour. Failing that, the principal yacht club in the port should give the time by hoisting and lowering the ensign at its own flagstaff.

Under the Merchant Shipping Act of 1894 an owner can be fined up to five hundred pounds for hoisting a special ensign aboard a yacht if he is a British subject and does not hold the necessary Warrant for the craft.

### THE WHITE ENSIGN

This is a plain white flag with the Red Cross of St George superimposed and the Union Flag in the upper canton at the hoist. It is worn by vessels of the Royal Navy when in commission, the Royal Yacht, and yachts belonging to members, other than naval members, of the Royal Yacht Squadron. In addition, Naval shore establishments commanded by a commissioned officer may wear this ensign and Trinity House vessels are also entitled to wear it at the masthead on ceremonial occasions when H.M. Ships are dressed overall.

### THE BLUE ENSIGN

This is a blue flag with the Union Flag in the upper canton at the hoist. By Admiralty Warrant Merchant ships may wear the undefaced Blue Ensign if they are commanded by a retired officer of the Royal Navy, or by an officer of any of the Naval Reserves, provided the crew contains a certain number of officers and men of any of the Naval Reserves. This ensign may be worn by yachts whose owner is a member of a yacht club carrying the privilege, and which have been granted through the club a Special Ensign Warrant.

### THE BLUE ENSIGN DEFACED

This is a Blue Ensign with some emblem superimposed at the fly. Royal Fleet Auxiliaries, certain ships under charter to the Admiralty and certain Naval yachts wear a Blue Ensign defaced with a yellow anchor at the fly. Craft belonging to H.M. Customs, H.M. Post Office, and certain other public offices of the United Kingdom wear a Blue Ensign with the badge of their office at the

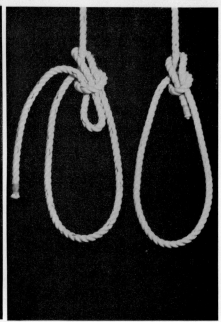

*Bowline on a bight*

*Bowline
with slip*

*Bowline*

*Plate 6*

*Fisherman's
bend*

Reef knot     Granny                Sheet bend
Sheet bend with slip

*Plate 7*

Rolling
hitch

fly. In addition yachts of certain approved yacht clubs holding Admiralty Warrants are also allowed to wear a Blue Ensign defaced by a badge of the club at the fly.

### THE RED ENSIGN DEFACED

This is a plain red flag with the Union Flag in the upper canton at the hoist, and defaced by some emblem superimposed at the fly. The National Flag of Canada is a Red Ensign with the shield of the coat of arms of Canada at the fly. Australian and New Zealand ships (other than those allowed by Warrant to wear a special ensign) wear as their colours the Red Ensign embodying their emblems. As in the case of the Blue Ensign, yachts of certain yacht clubs of the United Kingdom are entitled by Admiralty Warrant to wear a Red Ensign incorporating the badge of their club.

### THE RED ENSIGN

This is a plain Red Flag with the Union Flag in the upper canton at the hoist. Other than those ships and craft allowed by Warrant to wear a special ensign, ALL ships and craft of the United Kingdom are allowed to wear a Red Ensign plain and undefaced as their colours. Under the Merchant Shipping Act a registered yacht—that is a craft used entirely for pleasure and not for profit—if over 15 tons register is required to wear the Red Ensign on all correct occasions. A yacht under 15 tons need not be registered, but if owned by a British subject is still required by law to carry the Red Ensign on board and is also entitled to wear it on correct occasions.

### JACKS

This is the name given to a flag worn on a staff at the bow of a vessel when alongside or in harbour. Except on certain special occasions (such as when ships are dressed overall) it is not worn while under way. Ships of Her Majesty's Navy wear the Union Flag at their jackstaff and it is for this reason that it has incorrectly come to be called the 'Union Jack'. Naval ships of Commonwealth Countries wear either their national colours or a specially designed Naval Jack. Merchant ships usually wear their House Flag at their jackstaff. The origin of the custom in H.M. Ships of wearing the Union Flag as the Jack goes back to the days when 'men of war' and merchant craft looked much the same and in fact wore identical ensigns. It was desirable that they should be easily distinguishable, so an order was issued that the Union Flag should be worn as a Jack only by H.M. Ships of war. It is still in force.

### CLUB BURGEES

Every yacht club has its own burgee which is flown at the mainmast head of yachts belonging to its members. The design on the burgee is entirely up to the choice of the club provided it does not contravene any Ministry of Defence or Ministry of Transport regulation and cannot be confused with any other burgee, flag or ensign. Anyone chartering or being lent a yacht should use the burgee of his own club and not that of the owner.

The club burgee and the special flag of a flag officer of a yacht club correspond in principle to the commissioning pendant of one of H.M. Ships and the personal flag of a flag officer of Her Majesty's Fleet. In the Royal Navy these pendants and flags are flown continuously by day and by night whilst the ship is in commission and whilst the flag officer is in the exercise of his command. So if the analogy is to be strictly adhered to the club burgee or the special flag of a flag officer of a yacht club should also fly continuously by day and night whenever the owner is in effective control of his yacht, except when the racing flag is worn in its place. However, the custom now is that the club burgee is not flown by night in harbour, and the common practice is that it should be flown between 0800 (0900 in winter) and sunset when the owner is in effective control.

### FLAG OFFICERS' FLAGS

Frequently, in place of a club burgee, the Flag Officers of a club are authorised by the club to fly a special flag indicating their office. Generally the design is the same as that of the club burgee, but the Commodore will fly a broad (or swallow-tailed) pendant, while the Vice and Rear Commodores will fly the same pendant with one and two balls respectively superimposed in the area of the pendant near the hoist. In harbour, yachts so entitled will be seen to fly such flags continuously day and night from the mainmast head, and this is correct.

## RACING FLAGS

These are rectangular in shape and are flown at the mainmast head in place of a burgee immediately before, during and after an organised race. A racing flag is the private flag of the owner of a yacht and as such may carry any design to the owner's choice so long as it does not conflict with any existing design or regulation. However it is customary for yacht and sailing clubs to recommend a design and colour which is then known as the racing flag of that club. An owner should always use his own racing flag in his own boat and in any craft he may have chartered. A person racing a craft on behalf of the owner however should use the owner's racing flag.

Normally a yacht wearing an ensign should not do so while she is flying a racing flag. The ensign should be lowered when the racing flag is hoisted on the five-minute gun. It is a matter of courtesy for a yacht or other pleasure craft not engaged in a race to avoid hindering a yacht flying a racing flag. If for no other reason therefore its use should never be abused. On retirement from a race the racing flag should immediately be replaced by the burgee. Certainly in the small modern racing dinghy it is not always possible to have the means of hoisting and lowering the racing flag while afloat, and it has therefore come to be accepted that in such craft, from the time of leaving the shore immediately prior to a race until return to shore immediately on completion of a race, the racing flag may remain at the masthead.

It is not acceptable for the racing flag to become a permanent fixture in place of a club burgee as, alas, is sometimes seen to be the case in the smaller and more lax sailing clubs.

## PROTEST FLAGS

A protest flag is a signal that the helmsman of a yacht or dinghy intends to register a protest to the Race Committee against some observed action by an opponent which, in the opinion of the protester, has violated the rules of the race. Sometimes the club organising the race specifies the nature of the protest flag, but the Royal Yachting Association prescribes that it shall be either a flag or burgee or rectangular piece of material no smaller than the distinguishing flag customarily worn by the protesting yacht.

## HOUSE FLAGS

A House Flag is a private flag used by vessels in the Merchant Navy. It is a distinguishing flag for ships belonging to the same owner and is rectangular in shape and bearing colours and design to the owner's choice—usually some symbol appropriate to the 'line' operating the ship—but this must not conflict with any other flags or regulations. House flags are never used in craft wearing the White Ensign, and are not commonly used in sailing craft but may be seen in the larger power craft as they form a part of the suit of colours consisting of the ensign, house flag and burgee. The Royal Yachting Association Flag (square flag with broad blue cross on white background with a red diamond laid horizontally at the centre) is used by members of the R.Y.A. in harbour at the crosstrees (starboard yardarm), and comes within the category of house flags.

## SPECIAL FLAGS

Under this heading comes the Royal Standard, which is the personal flag of the Sovereign, certain flags used in the Royal Navy for signalling purposes and for distinguishing their commanding officers when afloat, and the 'Commodore's Flag' of the larger merchant shipping companies which is worn by their senior Master on being appointed Commodore of their fleet. Into this heading would come yacht club officers' broad pendants, the Union Flag and also the Pilot Jack—a Union Flag with a white surround—internationally recognised when hoisted at the foremast of a ship as indicating that a pilot is required. Flag 'Q', an all yellow flag, when hoisted singly would be considered a special flag since it is used by all craft upon entering her first foreign port of call or her arrival port on return, to indicate 'My vessel is healthy and I request free pratique'.

## SIGNAL FLAGS

The International Code of Signals (1969) contains twenty-six alphabetical flags, three 'substitute' flags, ten specially shaped numeral pendants and one specially shaped 'answering' pendant.

With this outfit one can make virtually any required signal by reference to the code book, but note that the Code was changed in 1969 and it is still possible to inadvertently obtain earlier copies containing out of date material.

Those interested in making flag signals at sea will find the excellent booklet 'Flags and Signals' which is published by Pelhams and produced by B.P. Yachting Books in conjunction with the Royal Yachting Association most lucid and useful. (It is *B.P. Yachting Book No. 2.*)

# 6

# Navigation in Small
# Open Boats

With one hand you flatten out and try to hold down a spray-soaked chart. In your mouth is the all important non-indelible pencil, and the other hand grasps the hand-bearing compass that you're squinting through to align on a wildly jumping object ashore. Your eyes smart with the salt, and your crew meanwhile, handling tiller main and jibsheet, shrieks at you to balance the . . . boat!

It's a far cry from visions of brass-hatted gods on ship's bridges holding sextants aloft while lesser minions hover above the deck-watches which are synchronised with that most holy of holies: the ship's chronometer!

Both are trying to do exactly the same thing: find out where they are. It's just the conditions and facilities that differ. We in our dayboats are the unlucky ones—we have to do it without what many a ship's officer would consider the essentials, such as a steady, windless and well-equipped chartroom.

Our small boat calls for greater skill and conjures up a sense of self-preservation that forces us to use every conceivable visual aid (like transits and odd changes in the appearance of the water).

Navigation is a fascinating study, and while the conditions in a dayboat allow at best a rough and ready check on one's progress —the accuracy of which falls in direct proportion to a rise in wind force—a basic knowledge of what it is all about is advisable. Any seaman worth his salt will at some time or another have taken a course in navigation or have made it his business to learn from an experienced hand how to read a chart and use a compass. It is because I know that in small boats there is a tremendous gulf between theory and practice of the art that I give this quick summary and a bit of practical chartwork. It will be short, and I hope lucid, and embrace only those facts we need to know in order to intelligently plan a short coastal cruise, and then to check while on that cruise if we are in fact keeping to a preselected track line.

## PUBLICATIONS

On a large craft where space is freely available it's easy to carry many large scale charts to provide complete overlapping cover of the proposed cruise, and one or two small scale charts which will together embrace the whole coast from start to finishing points. This can call for a bulky portfolio because the average Admiralty Chart measures 28 inches by 20 inches when folded into two equal halves—and they are best stored flat.

This is not practicable in a small boat where space is at a premium, but even so one ought to carry and familiarise oneself with the bare minimum number of large scale charts to cover the main harbours of refuge, and one small scale chart covering the whole cruise if possible.

As already indicated, the reader who is new to this game might feel it worth while obtaining Admiralty Chart No. 2565 (Trevose Head to Dodman Point including the Scilly Isles) for use during this section. It contains all the symbols referred to, and in addition embraces that area of the cruise covered in Chapter Seven.

To find which Admiralty chart covers which area of coast you look in the current 'Catalogue of Admiralty Charts and Hydrographic Publications' which, together with the chart itself, is available from your nearest Admiralty Chart agent. There is one in all the main ports. This catalogue shows the coastline of the British Isles with the boundary lines of the charts superimposed on it, so that you can at a glance select the one you need. In addition there are some excellent coloured charts available for yachtsmen from chandlers. I use the Admiralty charts because I am conversant with their symbols from my naval days. Admiralty chart No. 5011 gives the key to all symbols used on these charts, and this, too, is well worth buying because it opens the door to a wealth of information built into the charts which might otherwise be overlooked.

Two invaluable books for any seaman are Reed's Nautical Almanac for the current year (a veritable library in itself) and the 'Admiralty Sailing Directions' (commonly referred to as 'The Pilot') for the area of coast with which one is concerned. The latter gives a detailed description of the coast and off-lying dangers, with useful hints on any local tidal freaks and suchlike. Make sure however that it has been kept up to date by amendment from the various supplements issued from time to time. These detail all changes in features such as light characteristics, new wrecks, changes in buoy positions and alterations of leading-marks for guiding craft into harbours. These Supplements are available with the 'Pilot' from Admiralty chart agents.

In addition of course it will be necessary to know the times of High and Low Water at all the ports along the coast and the direction of flow of the tidal stream at any time. As already mentioned in Chapter Two, the former is obtained from Tide Tables, and I always use the Admiralty Tide Tables (Volume I) which covers all European waters and is available from the chart agents. It saves a lot of messing about getting hold of the locally printed tables which are often on sale at newsagents at the ports concerned—it is useful to have them all in one book, and very lucid instructions on how to use them are given at the beginning of the tables themselves. The latter—that is the speed and direction of the tidal stream—is available from either the chart itself (in somewhat limited form) or from one of the excellent 'Pocket Tidal Stream Atlases'. These are published to cover specific areas of the sea and coast, which were previously listed in Chapter Two. These booklets show in visual form, using arrows of varying length and thickness, the direction and speed of the tidal flow at Neaps and Springs for every hour up to six hours before and after High Water at either Dover or another major port in the region covered. You can therefore relate this to anywhere around the coast of the United Kingdom.

To summarise the publications:

One small scale chart covering the whole extent of the cruise (or two if this is not possible).

The maximum number of large scale charts showing the approaches to harbours of refuge along the coast which it is possible to carry without serious inconvenience.

Tide Tables for all the area you are covering on the cruise.

Pocket Tidal Stream Atlas for the area.

Admiralty Sailing Directions (Pilot) for the area.

So much for the publications, now for the tools.

### THE TOOLS YOU NEED

Just as with the charts, it is not so easy in a dayboat to carry anything like a full range of navigational gear which one would expect in the average coastal or offshore cruiser, but even in a dayboat I would regard the following as a minimum outfit of instruments required aboard before embarking on even a limited coastal cruise:

A good steering compass.

A small hand-bearing compass.

Parallel ruler of the sliding, not rolling type.

Pair of dividers.

Waterproof watch or clock.

Small but reliable aneroid barometer.

Pocket size transistor radio for weather forecasts.

Pencils (non-indelible) and soft rubber.

In addition, for use and fun, a cheap plastic sextant. They cost under £10 and can be invaluable for coastal work.

Plate 2 shows some of the above tools

### VARIATION

The world is a vast magnet with, unfortunately, the magnetic North and South pole not quite coinciding with the true North and South pole round which the world rotates. The compass needle, attached to the underside of the graduated card in the compass, points to the Magnetic North Pole which from our situation here in the British Isles appears to be a little to the West of the true North. So the compass card is slewed Westward of the True North. The exact value in degrees of this slewing is referred to as Variation: and rightly so, since it 'varies' according to where you are on the surface of the earth, and also according to the year. The fact is, this magnetic North Pole is wobbling about a bit somewhere up North under the crust of the earth and a little to the side of its rotational axis line.

To find the exact value of the Variation for one's position on earth and the year, you look at the chart you are using, and we had better take a look at chart 2565 now. You will observe, out in the sea, well away from the coast so that they do not obscure any features, three large circles formed by two concentric rings with graduations in degrees of arc round the circumferences. These are called 'roses' and you will see that the outside ring is graduated from 0 degrees at the top, round through 180 degrees at the bottom and on round to 360 degrees (or 0 degrees) again at full circle. You will also observe that the line joining these graduations of 0 degrees and 180 degrees lies parallel to the lines running up and down the chart. In fact, if you extended these lines they would eventually pass through the true North and South Poles of the earth. Remember it is around the line joining these two points that the earth rotates.

The inside circle is similarly graduated, but you will see that in this case the rather flowery arrowhead at 0 and 360 degrees is slewed some eleven degrees West of the true North–South line. This represents the compass 'rose' as it was in 1959—it states so on the line running across the centre of the 'rose'. In fact, across one of the roses on chart 2565, it states 'Variation 10 degrees 45 minutes West in 1959—decreasing about 8 minutes annually', in somewhat abbreviated form. So by simple arithmetic one deduces what the Variation will be for the current year. You will see that there is a very slight difference of variation on the three roses printed on this one chart.

But at worst we are playing around here with a correction of one degree or two, and since in our boat—an aquatic seesaw bobbing in the waves—we shall be very lucky if we steer a course within two and a half degrees of the one we are attempting, from a practical point of view we can ignore any correction to the variation and take that inner compass rose to be the graduated card on our compass itself. But it is obviously always an advantage to work from the latest edition of a chart since this may incorporate a more 'up to date' compass rose.

## DEVIATION

Most, if not all, ferrous metals have their own small magnetic field around them and if a compass is brought within range of this field it will be affected in some way and swing away from its alignment with the magnetic North and South Poles of the earth. This tendency due to the small local influences is referred to as Deviation.

Ideally one should remove all steel or iron outside the range of influence and this is generally taken to be about six feet. Things which come to mind are a seaman's knife on its lanyard round one's waist, the bag of spare shackles, the metal centreplate and rudder perhaps, and a host of other fittings about the boat, not forgetting the engine itself!

In practice of course it just is not always possible to mount one's steering compass or hold the hand-bearing compass over six feet off these disturbing influences. By all means one ought to do everything possible to eliminate it, but you may be sure there will be some deviation and it can be quite large—five degrees is not exceptional if your steering compass happens to be over the metal centreplate of a sailing dinghy. Bear in mind also that when the plate is raised and lowered the affect of the magnetic field on the compass will change. If, in addition, the rudder blade and rudder post also have a field of influence, every time you move the helm there will be some slight effect on the compass card. Don't despair!

In a ship, with full facilities for accurate navigation, a 'Deviation Card' is compiled, which is simply a notation of deviation experienced—East or West of the True North—when the ship is heading on any point of the compass. The whole ship is turned about an axis in the horizontal plane when she is sitting on a known line of bearing from two objects ashore (the two objects are kept exactly in line and the bearing by ship's compass is then compared with the known bearing).

To attempt to draw up a deviation card for a sailing dinghy is virtually a waste of time. Position of the metal centreplate and rudder already noted—not to mention the angle of heel at which you are sailing—will tend to influence the deviation and you would have to draw up a multitude of tables to cover all the different circumstances to get any accurate sort of answer. In a powerboat where any metal fixture is more or less static in relation to one's steering compass, however, it is well worth while compiling your own deviation card.

In practice, aboard really small boats such as we are thinking of, one resorts to visual checks. For instance, at some given moment, when you know exactly where you are in your boat, you will be able to find from the chart the accurate compass course to a distant point or place (it may be a headland or harbour or anything you choose). You simply steer your boat accurately down that line of bearing and compare your course with the known bearing. It soon throws up any significant error, and then one can allow for it. But remember this allowance will only apply on THIS PARTICULAR COURSE, and should be checked again after any large alteration of course because the deviation may have altered also.

### CONVERTING THE COMPASS COURSE TO TRUE COURSE AND VICE VERSA

Although in fact, as I have said, in a small boat one is well within one's limits of accuracy to work directly from the compass rose on the chart, and ignore the true rose which is the outer circle, on occasion it may be useful to know an infallible method of converting one to another.

It is quite simple: one just remembers the word:

### CADET

This is a mnemonic which helps one to remember that when converting a COMPASS (C) course to a TRUE (T) course EASTERLY (E) error (in the form of any Variation and Deviation) is ADDED (AD).

So think of the word with arrows drawn in as follows:

Naturally Westerly error is subtracted. So from that one mnemonic one can easily work out a Compass to True, or True to Compass course or bearing with either a total compass error of Westerly or Easterly value. It can come in handy.

The important thing is to indicate which of the circles on the rose one is using by putting the letter (T) for True or (C) for Compass after the course or bearing.

## STEERING COMPASS

In a small boat one needs a good steering compass which has a card that will still operate at a large angle of heel. There are on the market, small gimballed compasses but I have always found before long that in a dayboat a foot or a backside has 'terminated the gimballing'. I favour the racing dinghy type with about a three to four inch diameter card, clearly marked, which is intended to be let into the side decks but can easily be secured in a temporary housing somewhere on the centreline of the boat. (As illustrated in Plate 2.)

## THE HAND-BEARING COMPASS

When steering a course it is not accurate enough, or convenient, to try to sight along the card of your steering compass to obtain a bearing of some object on shore in order to 'fix' your position, so it is usual to carry another small compass fitted with a grip that can easily be held in one hand. The bowl of this compass incorporates two sights—one at each side diametrically opposite one another—which may be aligned with the object on shore. See Figure 36. The single pointed sight is kept on the far side, rather like sighting a rifle. Beneath the 'V' of the backsight is a vertical line and one simply reads off the bearing indicated on the compass card against this line.

On the more expensive hand-bearing compasses one may have a glass prism to refract the image of the compass card into the line of sight, but the principle is exactly the same. When using the hand-bearing compass hold it as far away from the steering compass as possible otherwise the magnetic influence between the two will cause a lot of deviation in both. Remember also that if you happen to be wearing steel rimmed spectacles it can be perplexing, if not disastrous!

You may wonder, having read the explanation of Variation and Deviation and how they affect your compass, why I have bothered you with them, since I've practically demolished them in the next sentence! The point is, you have to know they exist, and why they are caused, in order to be able to guard against and allow for them: crude though your available methods may be!

PARALLEL RULER

This is a device used for transferring a course line (or a line of bearing of an object ashore) either from or to the compass rose on

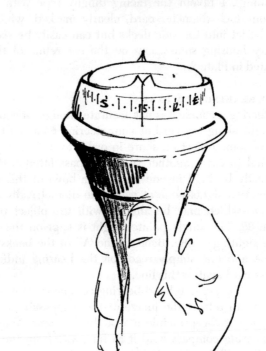

*Figure 36*

*Use of hand-bearing Compass*
*(The Church bears 150° by Compass)*

174

the chart, so that the value of the degrees of arc in relation to the magnetic North may be ascertained. It will be evident that if you wish to find out the compass course represented by a line you have drawn on the chart, you have to be able somehow to transfer that line without any error of orientation to the centre of your compass rose, so that you may read off the course on the outside graduations of the inner circle of the rose.

There are two types of parallel ruler which do this, one of which relies on a roller at either end. This type tends to slip very easily when used in small boat conditions. The other type consists of a wide transparent ruler the opposite edges of which are parallel. This is then cut longitudinally down the middle and the two parts so formed are held together by two pivotting arms which allow the two parts to separate while keeping their outer edges parallel. By alternately pressing on first one, then the other of the sides, and sliding the free side away while the ruler is locked to the chart by pressure of the other side, it can be slid over the paper while maintaining its accurate orientation. I much favour this latter type of ruler because any accidental skidding of the 'locked' side is more easily detected. Plate 2 shows this type.

## DIVIDERS

This is simply a two-pronged implement rather like a pair of drawing compasses except that there is a spike at both ends instead of a pencil at one. The points may be separated so as to span some six inches or so of a chart, and they are used to measure accurately the distances against the scale of degrees and minutes of Latitude up either side of the chart. See Plate 2.

## THE SEXTANT

There are those who will faint at the thought of taking a sextant aboard a dayboat. This instrument is bathed in an aura of mystery and associated with complicated mathematical calculations linked in some way with heavenly bodies.

If by a sextant one means an expensive and very sophisticated instrument, I agree: it would be sacrilege. But there are today on the market some very serviceable plastic sextants costing under £10 and though they do suffer from certain distortions affecting their accuracy they are, even so, very useful for one particular

method of finding one's distance off an object, the height and
position of which is marked on the chart.

It is called taking a 'Vertical Sextant Angle' and the principle
is simple. In any right-angled triangle, such as the one in Figure
37, if the length of AB is known, and the angle ACB is also
known, it is possible to calculate the length of BC.

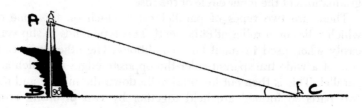

*Figure 37*

*To find the distance off by a vertical sextant angle*
*If you know the length of AB (height of the light) and the angle*
*ACB (taken with a sextant) you can calculate (or extract from*
*tables) the distance BC.*

The practical application of this is obvious. If the height of a
lighthouse above the waterline is known (AB) and the angle at
the observer's eye is known (ACB) then the distance off a point
vertically beneath the lighthouse can be calculated (BC).

The chart, or the 'Pilot', gives us AB. The sextant gives us
ACB—that is what a sextant does: it measures angles. Therefore
we can calculate BC. In practice no calculations are necessary, for
kind people have done them all in advance for us, and presented
them in tabular form. This table can be found in Reed's Nautical
Almanac under the heading 'Table for finding distance off with
sextant up to seven miles'. It comes under section VIII of the
book.

If you have this Nautical Almanac handy, you will see that the
height of the object above the waterline from forty feet up to
two thousand feet is given along the top of the pages, and in the
body of the tables a value in degrees and minutes of arc is presented in column form beneath each height. Having measured
the angle with the sextant one looks down the column beneath
the 'height in feet' of the object until you come across the nearest

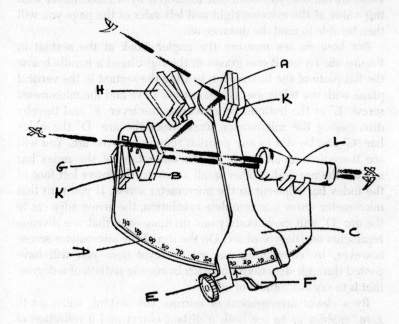

*Figure 38*

*The Sextant*

X   *Line of sight through unmirrored half of Horizon Glass.*
Y   *Reflected line of sight off Index Mirror and Horizon Mirror.*

A   *Index mirror*
B   *Horizon mirror*
C   *Index Bar*
D   *Arc (marked in degrees)*
E   *Micrometer screw (marked in minutes of arc)*
F   *Micrometer screw Engage/Disengage lever*
G   *Horizon shade (not in use on illustration)*
H   *Index mirror shades (not in use on illustration)*
K   *Adjuster screws on mirrors to eliminate 'index' and 'side' error*
L   *Sighting telescope*

value to the one you have just measured by sextant. Level with this value at the extreme right and left sides of the page you will then be able to read the distance off.

But how do we measure the angle? Look at the sextant in Figure 38. To use it one grasps in the right hand a handle below the flat plate of the instrument, holding the sextant in the vertical plane with the telescope 'L' against one's eye and the micrometer screw 'E' at the bottom. By squeezing the lever 'F' and thereby disengaging the micrometer screw from the arc 'D' the index bar 'C' can be slid to any position required on the arc. You will see there is a small arrow on the outer face of the index bar against the arc and another small arrow on the lower left face of the index bar adjacent to the micrometer screw. If you turn that micrometer screw one complete revolution, the arrow adjacent to the arc 'D' will move exactly one division—and that one division represents one degree of arc. On the rim of the micrometer screw, however, by completing one whole revolution, you will have passed through sixty divisions, each being one sixtieth of a degree, that is to say one minute of arc.

By a clever arrangement of mirrors, the sextant, when set to zero, enables us to see both a distant object and a reflection of the distant object exactly superimposed. If the sextant has no error, it will, when set to zero and sighted through the telescope at a distant object such as a lighthouse, reveal merely one light-house. If, however, with your left hand you commence slowly turning the micrometer screw, you will after a bit of practice see the reflected image moving in the vertical plane down below the actual object. The more you turn the screw, the further down it will go. It is important that the reflected image moves down. If you turn it in the opposite direction the reflected image will commence to move up, but then your readings will be what is termed 'off the arc' and you will probably fall into error.

The method by which the instrument effects this ghostlike movement of an image of an object away from an object is clever. Rays of light come from a distant object to you the observer using the sextant. One of the rays 'X' in Figure 38 passes through the unmirrored half of the horizon glass straight through the telescope to the observer's eye, so all the observer sees of that ray of light is the actual object viewed through the telescope and a plain window of glass. The other ray of light 'Y' however, coming from the same source, falls first on what is known as an index mirror 'A' fixed to the top of the index bar. From this it is reflected down to the other half of the horizon glass which half is mirrored. From here it passes through the telescope to the observer's eye. The instrument is so adjusted that when both arrows on the index bar are set to zero, (i.e. zero on the arc and zero on the micrometer screw) the reflected image exactly coincides with the object viewed. As the index bar is moved, however, you will see that the index mirror 'A' is moved also and this manifests itself to the observer by this strange ghost image moving slowly down away from the object.

Now imagine yourself to be viewing a distant lighthouse with your sextant set to zero. As you turn the micrometer screw, the 'ghost' lighthouse will move down toward the waterline and when in your estimation the centre of the lens of the 'ghost' lighthouse is exactly in line with the actual waterline, (see Figure 39) remove the sextant from your eye and read in degrees from the arc and minutes from the micrometer screw. What you are reading is the angle subtended by the lighthouse lens, your eye and the waterline, e.g. if the chart shows a lighthouse 220 feet in height and your vertical sextant reading is 1° 02'.0 of arc, by inspection of the table in 'Reed's', you will see that you are exactly two miles away from the lighthouse. If the height of your object is 150 feet and your sextant reading is 1° 46'.0 you will be eight cables, that is eight-tenths of a sea mile away from the object. You will notice that the table gives distances off only up to seven miles and the reason for this is that beyond such distances the angle subtended by the average lighthouse above waterline becomes too small for accuracy.

Looking at the sextant again, the major disadvantage of the cheap plastic variety is that being fairly flexible the mirrors 'B' and 'A' tend to move in relation to each other. You will appreciate that the very slightest distortion of that base plate will cause a very appreciable error throwing the reflected image 'way out' and I always check my sextant for the two major errors involved, namely index error and side error every time I use the instrument.

Index error is caused by either of the mirrors rotating about an axis at right angles to the plane of the instrument. It manifests itself when the sextant is set to zero by the reflected image not coinciding with the object but being either below or above it, i.e. in the vertical plane. It can be eliminated by a very slight adjustment of one of the adjuster screws 'K', having set the arc and micrometer screw to zero. One simply turns the screw in the required direction to make the two images coincide.

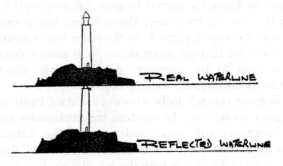

*Figure 39*

**Vertical Sextant Angle—how to align the images**
**The real waterline should divide the reflected lighthouse lens in half.**

Side error on the other hand is caused by either of the two mirrors rotating about an axis parallel to the plane of the instrument and manifests itself when the instrument is set to zero by the reflected image appearing to lie to one side, i.e. in the horizontal plane of the object viewed. Similarly this is eliminated by adjusting one of the other screws. You will soon find which by trial and error but I must warn you that you will have fun because the tendency is, unless you are very experienced, that while eliminating index error you are feeding in side error and vice versa. With a bit of practice, you will get the whole thing set up true and remember that when using the instrument for a vertical sextant angle you are mostly concerned with removing index error—the error in the vertical plane. A very small side error can be ignored. If one were using the sextant for sights on celestial bodies, such as sun, moon or stars, it would be absolutely imperative that all error was eliminated or at least known and allowed for, otherwise your observed position could be many miles 'out'.

THE CHART

A chart is a map of the sea and therefore the only land features included are those which will be useful to the navigator on the water. But the sea and the land are on the surface of a vast sphere —our world—so you will appreciate that when making a chart, just as with a map, there is going to be some sort of distortion resulting from the projection of this curved surface on to a flat plane. The methods of projection were dealt with in some detail in my book 'Dinghy Sailing', and sufficient here to merely remember that on the charts we shall be using around the coast of the British Isles the 'mercator' method of projection makes it imperative always to MEASURE DISTANCES AGAINST THOSE GRADUATIONS AT THE SIDE OF THE CHART and never along the top or the bottom.

In order to plot one's position on a chart some reference grid must be used. Horizontal and vertical reference lines are chosen and these are known respectively as parallels of latitude and meridians of longitude. Those running across the chart are parallels of latitude. Those running up and down the chart are meridians of longitude. By 'latitude' is meant the distance North or South of the Equator (which is taken as being Zero Latitude) in degrees and minutes of arc, and I think it is important here to understand exactly what is meant by a minute or degree of arc, and how this is linked to a sea mile.

If you draw two lines commencing at one point which is the centre of the earth, and let them form an angle with each other of one minute of arc (that is one sixtieth of a degree), those lines will cut the surface of the earth at two points exactly one sea mile apart. That is what is meant when we say that one sea mile is equal to one minute of arc. If the lines are moved so as to form an angle of one degree between them, then they will cut the earth's surface exactly sixty sea miles apart, since there are sixty minutes in one degree of arc. You will understand now why the sea mile is different to the land mile: the latter is a quite arbitrary choice of distance, the former is a measure of arc converted into linear distance at the surface of the earth. If the earth were of bigger radius, our sea mile would have to be longer!

I repeat then, by 'latitude' one means the distance in degrees and minutes of arc North or South of Zero latitude—the Equator. Looking at our chart you will see a parallel of latitude drawn in at 50 degrees North of the equator and another one at 50 degrees 20 minutes North. Only those two are marked on this chart, and the distance between them is 20 minutes of arc, or 20 sea miles. It is immediately evident that we are operating on this chart some three thousand sea miles North of the equator.

The meridians of longitude—there are six of them on our chart —give us our position (notice I do not use the word distance here) East or West of one prime meridian. It could have been any one, they would all have been equally as good, but the one chosen was that meridian which runs through Greenwich. The Greenwich meridian is therefore the zero meridian for our grid system, and on our chart the meridian 5 degrees West of Greenwich is the first to be seen on the right hand side. From then on a meridian is drawn on this chart every 20 minutes of longitude Westwards.

Now think about these meridians. Unlike the parallels of latitude they are not, on the surface of our earth, parallel to each other. In fact, they all join at each end at the True North and South poles. But the Mercator method of projection makes them APPEAR to run parallel to each other on the chart. So you should now see why a minute of longitude (that is measuring East and West) is by no means the same thing as a sea mile—except on the equator. This is why it is so important never to measure distances along the scale at the top or bottom of a chart. This scale is there simply so that we may, by reference to the grid system, indicate our position on the chart.

You have only to compare the length of one minute of arc of longitude with one minute of arc of latitude (one sea mile) to see the enormous difference.

Longitude is measured East or West of Greenwich (zero) meridian, and one must always remember to place these signs (E. or W. for longitude, N. or S. for latitude) when indicating a position on the earth.

By inspection of the chart therefore you will see that Trevose Head lighthouse is in position 50° 33'.0 N. and 05° 02'.1 W. You will notice that the latitude is placed first, then the longitude, and this is the correct way to present them. You will also notice the little sign ° denotes 'degrees' and the sign ' denotes 'minutes'. The longitude of Trevose is five degrees, two point one minutes

West of Greenwich, and you will note that the minute sign is always placed above the decimal point. If it were not so, one might mistake the reading for five degrees twenty-one minutes West. Do you follow?

The numbers printed all over the sea on this chart are soundings in fathoms (below the eleven fathom line in fathoms and feet), and it is important to understand that these soundings are the depth below chart datum.

### CHART DATUM

This, as you will have seen from the 'definitions' under the Chapter dealing with 'Tides', is the level below which soundings are given on the chart. The tide level very seldom falls—if ever—below chart datum. When a survey is undertaken of an area of the coast and sea, the depth of soundings has to be related to a fixed level. This is not easy because the level of the sea is constantly rising and falling by tidal effect, and it is only common sense from a safety point of view that soundings should be given below Low Water. But Low Water itself is a movable level—some tides are lower than others—so in practice a reference level is chosen below which the tide very seldom falls, and this is the level of chart datum. You may depend when looking at the chart that the soundings shown are the shallowest you will ever experience, even at the lowest of Low Water Spring Tides. Generally there will be a bit more water under your keel than is shown there.

### THE FATHOM

The fathom (six feet) is the unit chosen by which to measure depth. On chart 2565 any depth below eleven fathoms is given in fathoms and feet, the feet being indicated by the small figure just below and to the right of the fathom figure, like this: $6_3$ which means six fathoms and three feet. Charts will gradually embrace the metric system as they are reprinted, but for many years yet the old and honoured 'fathom' will be used in this country.

### THE METRE

Since, however, this unit of measurement will gradually appear to indicate depth on Admiralty charts and in many other fields of

183

our everyday life, it may be of interest to consider how the length has been arrived at. In 1791, the French Academy of Sciences decided that it would be useful to specify a unit of length which would be applicable in all fields. Two French scientists were therefore given the task of defining and accurately producing such a standard of measurement. It took them seven years to choose and measure with accuracy the 'metre' which is equal to one ten-millionth of the distance from the Pole of the earth to the equator. They used a section of a meridian from Barcelona in Spain to Dunkirk in Normandy, and a specially constructed platinum-iridium bar, not subject to expansion or contraction, is now kept in the Bureau des Poids et Mesures at Sevres near Paris, on which are two marks supposed to represent one ten millionth of the quarter of one earth meridian.

Unfortunately, it has been found that this minute fraction of the quarter of an earth's meridian does not, in fact, equal the length between those two marks, and since 1960 new standards have been adopted which I do not understand, and I'll bet you don't either. The metre is now $1,650,763·73$ wavelengths in vacuum of a transition between energy levels $2P_{10}$ and $5D_5$ of krypton-86 atom excited at the triple point of nitrogen.

Which is useful to know in a boat!

FATHOM LINES

Just as contour lines of height are marked on a land map, so on Admiralty charts contour lines of depth are indicated by a system of pecked lines. As you will see from chart 2565, when approaching the coast from deep water of over 20 fathoms, the 20 fathom line contour is indicated by a pecked line thus ·········-- The 10 fathom line thus ·-····-- The 5 fathom line thus --- --- --- and the 3 fathom line is given by a series of dots with the fine pecked shading coastwards. All these symbols are given, together with the symbols showing the actual nature of the shoreline (rocks, cliffs, sand, etc.) on chart 5011.

A sounding taken with a hand lead-line (see Figure 40) can be a very useful check on a position obtained by visual observation. Where a sandbank dries at Low Water (as on the Doom Bar at the entrance to the Camel Estuary) the height above chart datum of the exposed bank is given in feet with a line beneath, thus '4'.

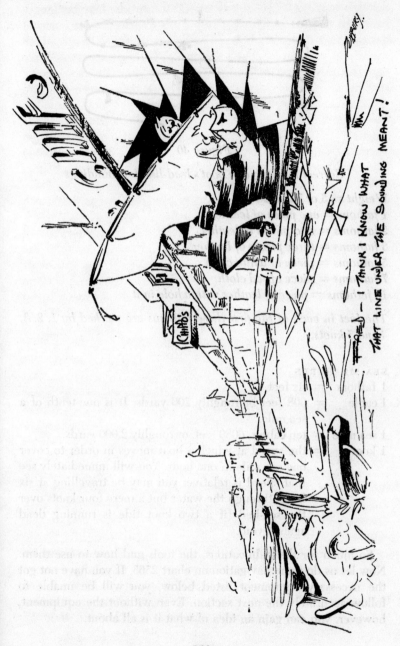

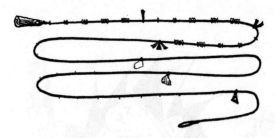

*Figure 40*

*Correct marking of a boat's lead-line for soundings*

*Weight = 5 or 7 lb lead*
*1 fathom = one piece of leather*
*2 fathoms = two pieces of leather*
*3 fathoms = three pieces of leather*
*5 fathoms = piece of white cloth*
*7 fathoms = piece of red cloth*
*10 fathoms = piece of leather with a hole in it*

*The feet in each of the first three fathoms are marked by 1, 2, 3, 4 and 5 knots.*

SEA MEASURES

| | | |
|---|---|---|
| 1 fathom | = | six feet. |
| 1 cable | = | 608 feet or roughly 200 yards. It is one-tenth of a sea mile. |
| 1 sea mile | = | ten cables, 6080 feet, or roughly 2,000 yards. |
| 1 knot | = | the speed at which a boat moves in order to cover one sea mile in one hour. You will immediately see that speed is relative: you may be travelling at six knots through the water but a mere four knots over the sea-bed (if a two knot tide is running dead against you). |

So much for the publications, the tools and how to use them. Now let us do some navigation on chart 2565. If you have not got the necessary equipment listed below, you will be unable to follow accurately the next section. Even without the equipment, however, you can gain an idea of what it is all about.

Chart 2565
Parallel ruler
Dividers (a pair of drawing compasses will do to improvise)
Soft but sharp non-indelible pencil
Soft rubber (preferably 'kneaded rubber'—it does not
    roughen the paper so much)

### THE COMPASS COURSE

There it is—the whole Western area of Cornwall and the
Scilly Isles—as though you were viewing it from a spacecraft
some thirty miles up. No atmosphere either to obliterate the
features.

Find the outer Quies rock in position 50° 32′.7 N. 05° 03′.6 W.
When you have located this you will see that it lies nine cables
(0.9 sea miles) West of Dinas Head. Don't cheat!

Now locate the Stones whistle buoy in position 50° 15′.6 N.
05° 25′.4 W. The exact position of a buoy on the chart is the
small circle at the bottom of the symbol. Check that you agree
this whistle buoy lies about 1½ sea miles North Westward of
Godrevy Island lighthouse. Notice that all points exhibiting navigational lights such as lighthouses, buoys, headlands, etc. are
marked with a mauve coloured blob for quick location.

Lay off a track line from the outer Quies rock to the whistle
buoy. To do this place one edge of your parallel ruler through
each and very lightly draw in with your sharp pencil a line to
join them. What is the compass course to steer in order to head
down that track line from Quies to the Stones buoy? I make it
230° by compass, read directly off the outer graduations on the
inner rose.

To find this I placed the bottom edge of my parallel ruler along
the track line and carefully transferred the upper edge to the
centre of the compass rose, reading off the graduation 230 degrees
on the outside of that inner circle. Ignore those graduations on
the inside of the circle; they have nothing to do with us. Notice
though that there was no need to transfer the BOTTOM edge of the
ruler to the centre of the rose on the chart. The less distance you
transfer that ruler the less chance there is of error creeping in
through skidding. So the course to steer by compass, in order to
head down that track line from the Quies to the Stones buoy is

230 degrees. This is not absolutely accurate because we have not allowed for the one and a half degree change of variation in the compass rose on the chart since the chart was printed, but as I said before, in our dayboat we shall be lucky if we steer within double that amount of any course!

Now if our area of water were the Serpentine, and our boat were motivated by power, and there was neither wind nor tide, it is just possible that after steering 230° Compass for 22 miles and 2 cables (check this distance with your dividers) we would be within hailing distance of the Stones buoy.

But we are in a bobbing boat on the open sea, in a wind and with a tidal stream running, and you may be sure that all these things are affecting our progress quite significantly.

How do we allow for this?

ALLOWING FOR THE TIDAL STREAM

The best thing to do here is to take an actual example. As you will have noted, that line which you have drawn on the chart, is called the track line. It is the line along which you do your best to travel, having allowed for wind and tidal stream which, naturally, will affect the course you have to steer. The good navigator checks constantly whether he is still on the track line by means of 'fixes' which we will deal with in a moment. First though, how do we arrive at a compass course to steer which allows for the tidal stream and may possibly keep us on that track line?

We need to know the direction and strength of the tidal stream in this area. Look on the chart in position 50° 19′.0 N. 05° 52′.0 W. You will see a letter 'N' contained within a mauve coloured diamond. Now look at the table of tidal streams up at the top of the chart, which you will notice are referred to the times of High Water at Devonport. The extreme right hand column, headed 'N' gives the direction and rate (strength in knots) of the tidal stream for every hour up to six hours before and after High Water at Devonport at that position. It is true that the position 'N' on the chart is not exactly where we are sailing, but this chart is not lavishly filled with tidal indication points on the North Coast of Cornwall, so if we have not a Pocket Tidal Atlas handy, it is the best indication we can get.

To simplify the problem let us imagine we are in a nippy speedboat capable of doing twenty-two knots, and the sea is flat calm. That means we are going to take one hour or thereabouts to travel from the Quies to the Stones buoy.

Assume that by inspection of our tide tables we have found that High Water at Devonport on the day in question is at 0900. It is now 1000 hours and we are at the Quies rocks, so already it is one hour after High Water at Devonport. Looking at the table on the chart you will see that at the point 'N' the stream is now running in a direction 168 degrees at 0.7 of a knot at Springs and 0.4 of a knot at Neaps, and this means 168° True—on the outer circle of the rose. It will be eleven o'clock in the morning by the time we are at the Stones buoy having taken one hour to get there. By that time—two hours after High Water at Devonport—the tidal stream at 'N' will be running 202°(T) at 0.9 of a knot (Spring) or 0.4 of a knot (Neap). We find, from inspection of the tide tables that it is near the 'top of' Spring tides.

We know therefore that in that area the tide will, from 1000 to 1100 on the day in question, be running on average somewhere between 168°(T) to 202°(T) at between 0.7 and 0.9 of a knot. If we settle for an average of 185°(T) at 0.8 of a knot we shall not be far out. Remember that means the stream is running TOWARDS 185°(T) at that position 'N' which is the nearest indication we have to our track line.

In other words, a chunk of wood floating well immersed in the water which happened to be, at 1000 a distance of 0.8 sea miles bearing 005°(T) from the Stones buoy will, during the next hour, drift with the water exactly 0.8 sea miles in a direction 185°(T) until it hits the whistle buoy at 1100.

It is obvious therefore that if we, in our boat which is speeding across that same water, wish to get to the whistle buoy we shall have to aim not for the buoy, but for that position 0.8 of a sea mile (8 cables) roughly North (in fact the reciprocal of 185°(T) which is 005°(T) from the buoy. Plot that point on the chart, using the outer rose, remember, because this tidal information is all related to the True North.

In order to steer for that point we shall have to lay off a course line joining the Quies to that point. Do this. I make it 231°(C), as near as no matter, and notice also that instead of having to speed for 22 miles 2 cables, we shall only have to cover 21 miles and 4 cables—the tidal stream has done the other bit for us.

In our fast speedboat this calls, as you have seen, for a very small correction to our compass course, but suppose we had been in a small dinghy doing a mere three knots it would have taken us about seven hours to do that trip, and IF the tidal stream had remained constant at the rate we have calculated that would have drifted us 5.6 sea miles in a direction 185°(T)—so instead of aiming for a point a mere eight cables North of the buoy we would have had to aim for a point five point six miles in a reciprocal direction to 185°(T) which is 005°(T). Plot that point 5.6 miles 005°(T) from the whistle buoy, and lay off another course to steer from the Quies. I think you will find that our course would have had to be 240°(C), and the distance we would have to travel through the water would be 17.4 sea miles. The tide would have done the rest for us.

But unfortunately the tidal stream would not have remained constant at 185°(T) during those seven hours, nor at the rate of 0.8 of a knot. In fact we would have had to either approximate a mean rate and direction over the whole seven hour period, or work out a 'one hour' tide triangle and correct our compass course each hour.

Even then we would still have made no allowance for the drift due to the wind—assuming that the wind was fair for laying that course. But wait—we have not finished yet: suppose the wind was adverse, and we were in a sailing dinghy and could not lay that course directly—we would have to sail close hauled, tacking constantly each side of our course line and allowing for the corrections as best we could. Now you understand what these long distance round-the-world sailors have to contend with when trying to calculate where they are heading, and why!

So much for the theory. The basic navigation we have been doing is called 'dead reckoning', because it is calculating what we ought to steer, taking into account as many factors which will affect that calculation as possible. It is not accurate in a small boat, unless we are extremely lucky, but we have to do it to the best of our ability because should fog come down while we are halfway down the coast, we shall have to rely on our calculations to get us safely to the nearest safe refuge. In practice, however, we constantly check on our position by 'fixes' obtained from objects ashore. So we find whether our inspired guess has been about right. In a small boat it seldom has.

## METHODS OF 'FIXING' ONE'S POSITION

There are a host of different methods of accurately fixing one's position while within sight of a coastline for which you hold a chart, but I am going to consider three, and their combinations, which are of most use to a dayboat sailor.

## TRANSITS

This is the most accurate and the easiest method. Two objects are said to be in transit with one another when they are exactly in line. Look at Figure 41 (Lower). Assume you wish to establish your exact position when running down that imaginary coast, to check whether you are in fact on the track line you have drawn on the chart before setting off.

You will observe that the lighthouse you have just passed is 'coming on' with the bluff cliffs behind it—this is the term used to denote that very shortly the two will be in transit. At the same time you will notice that a daymark is about to come into transit with a church also marked on the chart behind it.

It is quite evident that if you sail down the transit of the lighthouse and the cliff until you cross the transit of the daymark and the church, you will be exactly at the point on the chart where the two transits cross. You would then be able to plot them on the chart. Put a small circle round the point of intersection and note the time against it, or if in wet choppy conditions at least visually establish your position on the chart even if unable to plot it. It is, in our example, inside your track line, so something (probably the tidal stream) is setting you inshore. So you would steer a couple of degrees or so to seaward to gradually regain your track line and try to take another 'fix' in about a quarter of an hour to see if the correction has been enough.

## LEADING MARKS

Transits are a most useful method of determining an accurate approach into harbour, and for this reason the local authorities

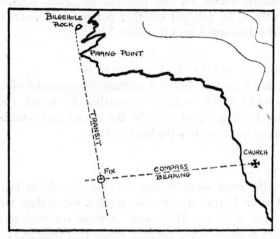

TRANSIT COMBINED WITH COMPASS BEARING

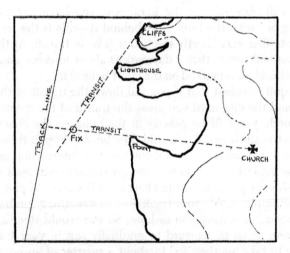

TWO TRANSITS GIVING VERY ACCURATE FIX

Figure 41

*Two methods of fixing one's position*

Clove hitch                    Timber hitch

Plate 8

Quick release hitch on cleat              Figure-of-eight

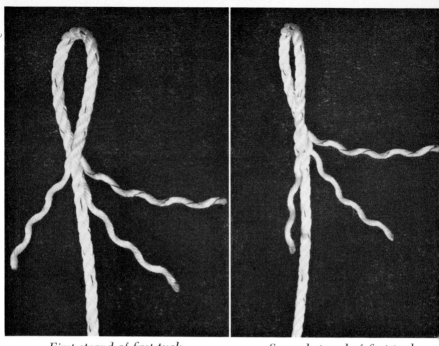

*First strand of first tuck*             *Second strand of first tuck*

Plate 9

*Third strand of first tuck*             *First tuck complete*

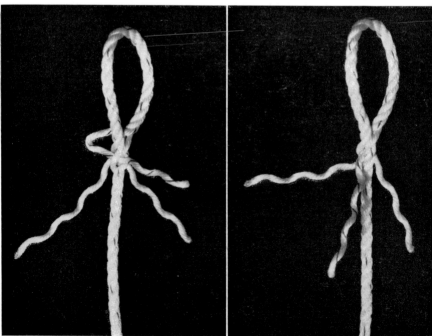

sometimes erect leading marks which are prominent and easily visible posts with generally a triangular or diamond shaped top-mark thereon. When in transit these leading marks will bring a craft into the entrance keeping her clear of any off-lying dangers. The 'Pilot' will give details of any such aids, and in the more important commercial harbours the line is frequently dotted in on the chart with the True bearing written alongside it. This forms a useful compass check, taking into account the variation which must be applied, before comparing the True with the Compass bearing. The method of converting a compass course or bearing to a true course or bearing (and vice-versa) has already been dealt with.

## TRANSIT COMBINED WITH COMPASS BEARING

Look at Figure 41 (Upper). We have a good transit, in this imaginary example, of Prang Point and Bilgehole Rocks, but nothing marked with which we can align that church. We could therefore sight the church and get a bearing on it by hand-bearing compass, remembering to give the compass card a chance to steady up on its magnetic field lines before taking the bearing —it takes longer than expected and is helped greatly by handling the instrument gently and smoothly rather than jerkily. Imagine it to be 090° by the hand-bearing compass. We would plot this on the chart by placing the parallel ruler through the centre of the chart rose and through the graduation 090° on the inner circle, then transfer this line through the church marked on the chart. Remember bearings are always from seaward, so we mustn't put ourselves five miles inland by plotting the reciprocal! Now draw in our transit line through Prang and Bilgehole, and there is the 'fix'. We would place a small pencil circle round the intersection point and put the time against it.

One point to note here: a bearing by small hand-bearing compass taken from a wildly moving dayboat is not very accurate. That transit line, however, which relies on no instruments, is absolutely accurate. Try to take your bearing by compass when the bearing line will intersect the transit line at RIGHT ANGLES. That way the margin of compass error will be the smallest possible when plotted to cut the transit line. In fact, any cross cuts to give a fix by compass such as we are considering are best made when the intersection angles are as near to a right angle as possible. It is common sense when you think about it.

## TWO OR MORE COMPASS BEARINGS

Often there is no convenient transit of two objects which are marked on the chart, so one must simply take two compass bearings, plot them, and circle the point of intersection, but if possible a bearing from a third object on shore should be taken simultaneously with the other two. This will always result in a small triangle at the intersection area of the three lines, unless you are fantastically lucky and get them all to coincide. This triangle at the intersection of the three lines is called a 'cocked hat' and the mean of the three intersections—the centre of the triangle—should be taken as one's position. See Figure 42 (Upper). Guard against taking two objects which are nearly on reciprocal bearings, such as 090° and 260°, because if you think about it the smallest error in the compass will throw the points of intersection a long way out. They're useless.

## VERTICAL SEXTANT ANGLE COMBINED WITH TRANSIT OR COMPASS BEARING

It will be apparent that by taking a vertical sextant angle, as previously described, you establish a distance off an object, but your position can lie anywhere on a circle of that established radius. Combine this with a transit line of the object you are sighting and some other object marked on the chart and you immediately know your position.

But take care here. The transit is best taken of the object you are sighting with the sextant, and something else, otherwise a situation as depicted in Figure 42 (Lower) can result, and then—where are you, at A or B?

If you cannot get a transit, it is best to take a compass bearing of the object you have sighted with the sextant immediately you put the sextant down—because don't forget you are moving all the time. Then you have a distance off and a bearing.

Combinations of all these methods are possible, and of course it is also invaluable to check any 'fixes' by a sounding with the lead-line. Never miss any opportunity to check and double check your position. It is absolutely essential if visibility suddenly

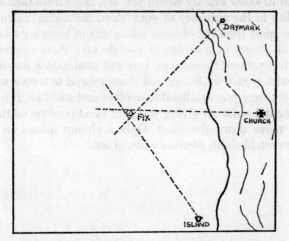

THREE COMPASS BEARINGS GIVING FIX WITHIN 'COCKED HAT'

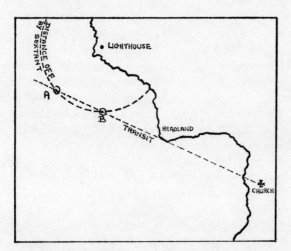

POSSIBLE ERROR IF USING A VERTICAL SEXTANT ANGLE COMBINED WITH A SEPARATE TRANSIT. WHERE ARE YOU... A OR B ?

*Figure 42*

*Two more methods of fixing one's position*

closes in to know exactly where you are, since from then on your safety lies in the accuracy of your 'dead reckoning' calculations.

Quite apart from the obvious advantage of knowing where you are at all stages of a cruise, if you do take these opportunities when they present themselves, you will soon gain a sort of 'sixth sense' with regard to distance off shore related to time it will take you to get from one headland to another and suchlike. It is almost like a mental radar set giving you your exact position on the chart as you move down the coast. Only a chump misses an opportunity to establish his position when at sea.

# 7

# The Cruise

The object of including these two days of an actual cruise is to help the reader to apply some of the theory we have been considering. Though it embraces only two days of a two month cruise, the area of coast chosen does represent the most hazardous of the trip and therefore calls for the greatest forethought. Many of the situations can apply to anyone venturing off an exposed shore, even if it be for a mere afternoon's jaunt.

ADVANCE PLANNING

Careful forethought does not detract in any way from the enjoyment of a coastal trip, no matter how short, so the attitude 'Let's go anyway and see how things develop' should be thrown overboard.

When planning any cruise one of the most important aspects is the end of it. Any chump can set off—the skill lies in arriving safely at one's destination. This means arriving to suit the state of tide and (in a dayboat) daylight. I do not consider it an acceptable risk to be at sea off a strange coastline after dark in a small open boat. Should the weather deteriorate and correct assessment of conditions on shore and round the horizon become impossible, then the margin of safety has already shrunk greatly. Give yourself plenty of scope in case of delay during the passage. Safe points of refuge must be studied on the chart bearing in mind the wind direction and the type of sea and swell which is running. Be aware constantly of the nearest place affording shelter and this need not, of course, be a harbour or inlet; any place where you may land without danger to life (though it may mean

197

'writing off' your boat) is worth all the gold of Midas when conditions have become too much for you to cope with.

Understand that the essential difference between coastal cruising in a dayboat and a larger craft lies here: for the larger seaboats, often the safest action when caught in rapidly deteriorating conditions is to stand offshore as quickly as possible. It may result in discomfort for the crew but the boat can survive. Our small dayboat however cannot survive in a rough sea, so shelter must be reached before conditions make it too dangerous to approach the refuge ashore. This is a fundamental difference which makes the whole margin of safety much smaller.

It is a wise practice to visualise the coastline within one hour's reach of your present position as being divided up into 'red' (danger) and 'green' (safe) areas. For the small boat man the red areas will occur on the weather side of headlands and within a mile or two offshore of the headland itself. Lee shores anywhere should be seen as tinged red because the seas, and probably swell also, will be breaking thereon. Offlying shallows and rocks of course come within the red bracket; the difference in the sea's surface when one passes over a localised shallow bank can be of more than academic interest to a dayboat.

Green areas will come on the lee side of headlands, along a weather shore, and of course inside harbours, creeks and estuaries though the latter may have a bright red splash across the mouth— the sandbar.

In all but really fast craft the tidal stream should be utilised, and opportunities to eat must be considered because a cold and hungry crew is much less efficient or capable of dealing with adversity. Here let me say that alcohol at sea is just 'not on'. Certainly it can buoy you up when feeling depressed or apprehensive, but it gives you an altogether false courage which can lead to a wrong appraisal of a situation. It also lets you down with a bump after a very short time into an even worse state of depression.

ADDITIONAL CRUISE EQUIPMENT

In addition to the 'catastrophe' and 'utility' gear listed in Chapter Four and the navigational items dealt with in Chapter Six, for this cruise I took along as an emergency liferaft two inflatable airbeds. These both had stout eyelets at one corner to which I attached a light line for securing to myself and my crew, otherwise such buoyancy tends to part company in any wind! A piece of marine plywood (varnished) served many purposes: chart table on board and food table ashore, but primarily it was to use as an emergency patch on the hull. It is unlikely that any worthwhile repair could be effected while under way, but at least having run for that deserted beach I could then make her seaworthy until the next Port. Hammer, a few copper nails and selection of screws, and a tube of Seelastik (composition like very pliable putty) went into the Bosun's bag, together with a first-aid kit, waterproof electric torch, and the gas operated foghorn and small collapsible radar reflector. In the lugger I have stowage space for a second fisherman's anchor and additional sixty feet of warp, and my sea-anchor forms a permanent item of the boat's gear.

### RESPONSIBILITY TO THE SHORE AUTHORITIES

Always bear in mind before embarking on a cruise that you and your crew are not the only people concerned. Whether you like the idea or not, shore authorities are involved the moment you set sail because if anything untoward occurs they are the people who will be called upon to do something about it. Harbour-masters, Coastguards, and the Royal National Lifeboat Service together with other rescue organisations may be alerted due to your negligence, and you cannot blame them if, having been so alerted, they take seamanlike steps to start 'search and rescue' operations even though in the event it may be quite unnecessary. Before even going up the coast and back on a day's jaunt you should inform a responsible person ashore. This can be just a friend or member of the family, but be quite sure that they know what the boat looks like, her length, colour and shape, hull or sail number and name, and the number of persons on board. Make quite clear what your intentions are.

Always inform the local Harbour Master before leaving a port to which you are not returning of your next intended port of call, and if for any reason you then decide to put in somewhere other than that port, make it your business to inform him where you are otherwise a potential 'search and rescue' situation is ripe for development.

Similarly you should always report your arrival to the Harbour Master immediately. It is to him the authorities will refer if alerted. This is only common sense: the first thought to enter your mind if you get into serious trouble will be 'Does anyone know where we are?' Somebody *ought* to know where you are so that when you are missed the authorities can pinpoint the search area. The Coastguard refer to the Harbour Master if an alert is raised, and this organisation maintains some 150 lookout stations round our coastline, about one third of which maintain regular watch. The rest are manned only in bad weather conditions but all stations are on the telephone and they form the focal point of all action, providing the link between the various rescue organisations such as lifeboats, inshore rescue boats, rescue helicopters or R.A.F. Coastal Command search planes. To contact them on shore you simply dial 999 and ask for the Coastguard. You will be connected to the nearest District Headquarters who will alert the appropriate coastal station if necessary.

A system of Coastguard surveillance for boats undertaking a coastal passage is available. Application is made for a form CG 66 either in person, by telephone or by writing to the local District Headquarters (given in the Telephone Directory). This form records details of your proposed passage, a brief description of the boat and method of identifying her so that Coastguards along the route can keep watch. There is no charge for this service, but do be sure always to report your arrival or any change in plans.

With the foregoing in mind let us do the planning and carry out the first two days of a cruise I undertook in June 1970. It will be best first to state my intention with regard to the range of the cruise, the requirements by way of a boat, and then set about compromising to get the best craft for the job as I saw it. You may not agree with the solutions and compromises I settled on, but it will be a good exercise in seamanlike forethought just knowing in your own mind why you don't agree!

We are to start from Rock in the Camel Estuary opposite Padstow on the North coast of Cornwall. The intention is to coast Westward round Land's End, then strike Eastward to explore the creeks and harbours of the South Coast before retracing our steps back to Rock. In this book we will go as far as Mousehole just South West of Penzance, and I will leave you there. The area is covered by Admiralty Chart No. 2565 with which you are now, I hope, familiar.

First decision then: to take a crew, or 'go it alone'? This had to be settled before choosing a boat. Here I was lucky; my wife knows the ropes in a boat, is not seasick, has a cool head and doesn't panic when things go wrong. What is more we get along famously together. If you ever expect to find more than these four basic attributes in one crew member, you'll be disillusioned! The idea appealed to us both, so that was settled.

The requirements were as follows:

(a) The boat had to accommodate two in moderate comfort.
(b) She had to be primarily a sailing craft because I'm a sailor, but not one of those dyed-in-the-canvas types who spurn the thought of an engine.
(c) She had to carry an auxiliary motor of sufficient power to give at least three knots in a lumpy sea with brisk headwind, and four to five knots in calm water.
(d) She had to be light enough for the two of us to manhandle down a sloping beach without slipping any discs. I wanted to land on exposed beaches when sea conditions permitted, and take the bottom in harbours, but when beached I did not want to be completely at the mercy of the tides.
(e) As well as landing on shallow beaches I wanted to steal up quiet creeks where there might be a mere foot or two of water.
(f) Despite these considerations of size, draught and weight, she had to be a first-class seaboat with plenty of inherent stability and buoyancy, able to survive when properly handled in winds up to force 7 on the Beaufort Scale.

It's not asking much, is it!

Here is the boat I chose, after a great deal of searching; the Drascombe Lugger. See Figure 43.

Here are the reasons why, item by item.

(a) Since we had no intention of making night passages in which it would have been necessary for one of us to sleep while under way, a cabin was not essential. An airbed each side of the centreboard case and a stout tent rigged over the whole boat, lapping under the gunwales, would suffice. It proved very warm and comfortable and eliminated the need for top-hamper when under way with the resultant windage which I loathe in any boat. The less there is above the waterline once one has adequate freeboard, the better.

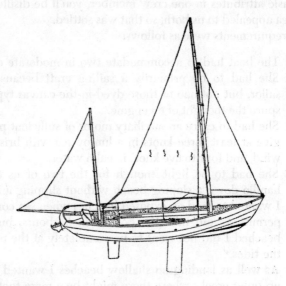

**Figure 43**

*The Drascombe Lugger*
*Length 18 feet. Beam six feet three inches.*
*Draught (plate up) 10 inches. (Plate down) 4 feet.*

(b) She carried three sails of total area 120 square feet. Rigged as a gunter yawl it was a simple matter to choose any combination of the three depending on one's need. Very important: she carried enough canvas for a moderately good performance on all points of sailing but not so much that one had to be constantly reefing. She carried all sail happily in up to force five winds.

(c) A four horsepower longshaft Mercury outboard fitted neatly down the trunking aft of the mizzen mast. This gave me four and a half knots in calm water and about three knots in a headwind with sea running. Equally important; it was economical on fuel, using about one gallon every two and a half hours at cruising revs. I could carry a good reserve—around fifteen hours running time. With a weight of 55 lbs I could easily carry the motor to and from the boat.

(d) The all-up weight of the wooden version of this Drascombe Lugger is around 750 lbs. This is just about the limit two of us could manage down a sloping beach.

(e) Her draught is ten inches with both rudder blade and centreplate raised. The longshaft outboard when lowered drew fourteen inches. If it had to be raised we could still carry on up those shallow creeks under oars. She rows very well indeed.

(f) Her lines were superb. She would obviously be a dry boat with good inherent stability, augmented by the 115 lb half-inch thick centreplate and the metal rudder weighing 28 lbs. The only modification I made to the standard boat produced by Kelly & Hall, the builders, was the provision of watertight hatches to seal off the large bow and stern lockers to make her permanently buoyant if swamped. A boat of this size would be exciting in winds above force six on the Beaufort Scale and I felt instinctively that she had as good a chance of coping with worse conditions as any other craft I had looked at.

The tent was made to my own measurements. The mast was used as a ridgepole, being supported on two light crutches and it worked splendidly, chiefly because it was only the work of a moment to lower the main mast which pivoted on deck. The mizzen mast, being unstayed, just lifted from its socket.

What do you think of her? She filled all the requirements I had imposed. It is the work of a moment to drop the mainsail even when running before the wind, which is a big advantage over a Bermudan rig. Being loose footed in the main the chances of an accidental gybe were also removed. Remember that out along the coast a boat tends to roll and yaw more than in calm water which is all conducive to gybing. The rig is slightly less efficient than a Bermudan sail when working to windward but I was quite prepared to accept this in exchange for the all-round safety. During the cruise she proved to be perfectly balanced under mizzen and jib alone and could be steered quite easily with the rudder unshipped by trimming these two sails. At first I found it awkward having to unship the rudder well out in deep water before landing on any shallow beaches, but if running into the beach she could be steered with an oar used as a sweep over the stern. She has a crutch fitted for that purpose.

I do not wish to imply that the lugger is, in my opinion, the only boat which might fulfil the requirements. I have spent thousands of hours in fairly high performance cruising dinghies such as Wayfarers. Some of these are excellent dinghies and have completed a few epic cruises with skilled crews. But I would not group them under the heading of 'open seaboats' because the sort of seas I was prepared to meet off the open coast would soon have taxed a normal crew beyond acceptable limits in such craft. They require continuous sitting-out if capsize is to be avoided. If asked to generalise I would suggest that any boat of sixteen feet in length and under is best kept to areas within immediate reach of sheltered water.

## PLANNING THE DAY'S SAIL

So being in all respects ready for sea, we find ourselves at Rock waiting patiently for a force six wind to ease. It has been blowing from the South East for the past three days, and the weather map from yesterday's 'Times' gives a good indication why. Look at Figure 44.

This gives the situation forecast for midday yesterday—the latest we have available at this moment. The weak occluded 'low' South of this country has been approaching from the West giving us the South Easterly winds which would be expected at a position of about two o'clock on the clock face of that isobar 1008. But the strength of these winds has been far greater than might be expected from the spacing of the isobars on this map. The reason is not hard to find. A 'high' of 1024 millibars is sitting just North East of us over the Baltic, and we can guess that the clockwise circulating wind on that isobar 1024 and 1016 to the Eastward of England has been joining with and augmenting the South Easterly wind caused by the 'low'. The important thing is that there are no bunched-up isobars out there to the West of that 'low'. In other words there is a slack pressure gradient out there so we should not expect any violent weather, and since the barometric pressure has remained fairly steady over the British Isles the weather is unlikely to change much. We can expect, in this stable situation, local convectional effects such as sea-breezes,

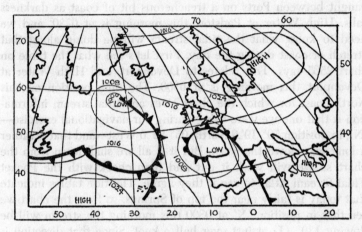

*Figure 44*

*Weather situation as forecast by the 'Times' weather map for noon on the day before sailing from Rock.*

but areas of calm wind are likely. As the 'low' moves more Eastward (which we expect) we have been anticipating a backing of the wind more North Easterly. You would expect this in a position of about eleven o'clock on the face of that 'low'.

Force Four on the Beaufort Scale is the maximum wind strength in which I would leave harbour in a dayboat. If there was any chance of this freshening I would, even then, not venture off an exposed coastline. This morning the 0640 Shipping Forecast on 1500 metres (Radio 2) has just given North East winds force 3 to 4 in the Lundy area, moderating toward evening, and there is nothing violent in the Plymouth or Portland, Fastnet or Sole areas, so evidently our interpretation of yesterday's weather map has been fairly accurate. Indeed, at this moment the wind is from the North East about force 4 to 5 and moderating. No sailor could ask for a fairer wind for running down the North coast of Cornwall. We must use it to the full, so let us do our final thinking.

First, examine the state of the tide. Our possible destinations for today are either Newquay some twelve miles away, or St Ives, about 32 miles down the coast. We shall not get any farther than that today because to push on past St Ives will be to risk getting caught between Ports on a treacherous bit of coast as darkness falls. High Water at Padstow this morning is at 0730, and we need to know what the tidal stream will be doing along that stretch of coast during the day. First let's see what the table on chart 2565 says. This relates to Devonport, and High Water at Devonport this morning is at 0800. The only position on this North coast for which the chart gives any tidal stream information is that one we were using during our navigational exercise— 'N', in position 50° 19'.0 North, 05° 52'.0 West—and that is rather a long way down the coast. But it is all we shall learn from the chart so we will work it out and then check with the Pocket Tidal Stream Atlas to see if they agree. The tide tables indicate that today is fairly near the top of Springs, so from the chart we see that in position 'N' at 0800 this morning the stream will be flowing 139° (T) at just over half a knot. Since that direction is almost straight towards the shore we can assume that the direction of flow is just on the change, and indeed one hour after High Water at Devonport, which will be 0900 this morning it has already swung round to 168° and increased a little to 0.7 knots. At 1000, 1100 and 1200 today it will be running 202° (T), 227° (T) and 235° (T) respectively and increasing to a maximum of 1·1 knots. The stream does not start running against us until four hours before High Water at Devonport this evening which will be at 1615 when it swings to a direction 025° (T). This is splendid: we can expect to carry both tide and wind behind us for most of the day.

We will check those figures with the Pocket Tidal Stream Atlas for the English and Bristol Channels. This publication relates all times to High Water at Dover which today is at 1320. To make it easy we will take that to be 1330. 0830 this morning will therefore be five hours before High Water at Dover, and turning to page four of the Atlas we see that five hours before H.W. at Dover there will be a flow at this estuary mouth of just under one knot in a direction down the coast towards Land's End. What is more, by inspection of the following pages in the Atlas we find we shall experience this favourable tidal stream until about 1530 today, when it begins to swing back up the coast at about half a knot. So there is broad agreement between the charted information and the Tidal Atlas, and we can, on average, assume that just under one knot will be added to our speed over the sea-bed until roughly 1500 this afternoon. What is the time of Low Water at Newquay and St Ives? This turns out to be at 1325 and 1315 respectively today, and High Water at St Ives this evening is at 1921.

So the sum of it all is that we shall have a favourable tide until 1530, and Low Water farther down the coast occurs at about 1330.

With this wind I know the lugger can be expected to do about four knots and allowing one knot favourable tidal stream this means we can be off Newquay around 1030 provided we get to this estuary mouth by 0800 and if (it's a big IF) the wind remains constant, we could be off St Ives by about 1430 this afternoon. The tide will already be rising at St Ives.

(In case the reader thinks I have manufactured these calculations to suit the first day, let me say now that this was exactly the situation on the morning we set off—June 6th 1970. If you have that year's Tide Tables handy you can check.)

One more cautionary thought before we sail: supposing the wind backs yet more and freshens from the North, despite the forecast? It will make this North coast a lee shore all the way to Land's End. If conditions become too much for us to cope with we can certainly get a good lee under Trevose Head but conditions are unlikely to deteriorate so soon—we shall only just have got under way. South of Park Head some three miles beyond Trevose will also give a lee but I don't like the look of those off-lying rocks and the coast is cliffbound with rocky foreshore. Not a very happy place to shelter from a strong Northerly, and regardless of the wind direction I know that the prevailing swell along this coast rolls in from the Westward. It shallows up from nine to three fathoms in a very short distance to the South of Park Head and the swell might be building up in height to break with force on those cliffs. Newquay itself lies on the weather side of Towan Head with a Northerly wind . . . it doesn't look too good at all if that wind does freshen from the North, for we might be arriving at Newquay at about half tide and falling and it may not be the best of harbours to take the beach or even anchor near the entrance. We will look it up in the Admiralty 'Pilot' for the West Coast of England. I quote: '. . . the tidal harbour, which dries, is contained within North and South Piers. Within the harbour a partly-demolished jetty projects Northward from the Southern side, parallel with the South Pier. In 1929 the harbour was abandoned and closed to all shipping except small craft with local knowledge. *Caution*: A vessel should not attempt to enter the harbour when there is a ground swell on, nor during an onshore gale as the sea breaks heavily off the entrance and for some distance outside.'

The Pilot says nothing useful about that shallow creek just South of Newquay except that it is available for coasters at Spring tides. It is quite evident from the chart that it dries out at low water for the whole creek is shaded with fine pecking. You may be sure there will be a surf at the entrance with a Northerly wind. Not very comforting: make no mistake this North coast of Cornwall is a rotten place to be caught out in a small boat!

Take a further look down the coast. St Agnes Head and Portreath are useless with a Northerly wind and there would certainly be a good old sea running on the weather side of Godrevy Point and the island off the Point, not to mention those ghastly Stones rocks extending some two miles offshore. We will see what the Pilot says about St Ives Harbour. I quote again:

'The tidal harbour of St Ives is contained within main or inner pier, a stone pier which extends Southward from the South-Eastern side of the Island and West Pier, which extends Eastward from the coast just North of St Andrew's Church in a direct line toward the outer end of main pier. The distance between the outer ends of the piers is three-quarters of a cable. The depths in the entrance vary from about 15 feet at High Water Springs to 9 feet at High Water Neaps; within the harbour the depths are about one foot less.

'The bottom of the harbour is composed of sand, with a slight coating of shingle or ballast. Small craft which can lie aground can be accommodated and are secure from all the winds. They are secured head and stern with their bows to large iron posts above High Water and their sterns to mooring buoys.'

Well, thank Heaven for that! It looks as if St Ives is going to be our first real place for shelter if the wind backs Northerly. I'm off to 'phone the local 'Met' man at St Mawgan R.A.F. to see what they have on the books...

... and it's evident that he expects the wind to moderate as the day grows older, probably falling light by this evening. If it falls away we have plenty of fuel. Get that track line plotted on the chart from a position halfway between the Bull and the inner Quies rock off Trevose Head down the coast to the centre of the channel inside Godrevy Island. With tide behind us and wind also we have no need to make allowances for a course to steer: 226° by compass will keep us on it. The Stones North West of Godrevy Island will present the main navigational hazard after leaving Trevose Head but the Pilot indicates that the channel inside the Island is 150 yards (¾ cable) wide with a least depth of ten feet. We will assess the situation there when approaching the area to decide whether to go through that channel or outside the Stones whistle buoy.

It is now 0730 and we want to be round Stepper Point and heading for Trevose by 0830 to pick up that favourable stream. The bar at the mouth is quiet—High Water is the safest time to pass over it, and we are going to motor to the estuary mouth for two reasons: firstly if this wind is going to die I don't want to waste what there is of it in beating North out of this creek, and secondly I'm a great believer in testing all gear. If trouble is going to develop with the outboard (it does sometimes happen!) this twenty minutes will give it a chance to declare itself. No point in getting sail on her until we are at Stepper Point. It's a splendid morning, brisk wind, clear sky and good visibility. With the wind in the same direction as the tidal stream we shall have a dry passage down, with little sea running and a 'soldier's wind' abaft the beam. I am hoping out there that the wind will have just enough Easterly in it to allow us to run down that long stretch on a broad reach Port tack, rather than goosewinged all the way; much more satisfying to have the wind on a quarter and certainly faster. The steering is easier too.

CHECKING THE COMPASS

0815 and Stepper is abeam to Port. This is an excellent opportunity for checking the steering compass for any big error. Since we shall be running with the metal centreplate one quarter down from Trevose Head onward, put it into that position now prior to checking the compass so that any Deviation will come into play. What would a line on the chart drawn through Trevose Lighthouse and the North face of Stepper Point represent as a compass course? I make it 262° by compass rose. I'm going to motor North out of the mouth until I first see Trevose Lighthouse come open of Stepper then turn and head straight for Trevose light and check my course. Certainly by my steering compass it is between 260° and 265°; in this lop one cannot get it nearer than that, and it is good enough for our purpose. So we can feel happy that our compass is accurate, and even though this is not quite the course we shall be steering from Trevose to St Ives, it is near enough not to involve any change in Deviation so we will not need to check again at Trevose.

There is a daymark—it is a tall stone tower—on Stepper which the chart indicates to be 272 feet in height (shown by the figure in brackets). Before hoisting sail we will take a vertical sextant angle on that tower and a compass bearing to give a point of departure from which we can check our speed during the day, but a point worth noting here; you remember that when using a lighthouse for taking the vertical sextant angle it was the centre of the lens which was brought down to the waterline? In this case it will be the very top of the tower. I read off an angle of 6° 20'.0, and Reed's Nautical Almanac supplies a table for objects 270 feet above High Water, which is near enough. Do you agree that makes us four cables (800 yards) away from the tower? The bearing by my hand-bearing compass is 190°. Plot that on the chart and remember that the distance has to be measured from the tower itself and not from the shoreline adjacent: it makes a deal of difference if the object you're sighting happens to lie half a mile inland! Note here also that the bearings of objects ashore

210

are ALWAYS given from seaward. Note that position and the time in the log for today as follows:

0820: Stepper Daymark bearing 190° by compass distant 4 cables. Set course 260° (C) for Trevose Head.

Now to get all sail on her.

OFFLYING SHOALS

So here we are off the coast, and what a different world it is from back there inside the estuary. On a sunny day like this the water, being really deep, is inky blue black and as we look around the true scale of things is brought home to us. The limitless expanse of water to the North, the unbroken view of sky from horizon to horizon East and West of us, and as a backcloth to it all those high black cliffs close to the South skirted with white foam. There is more swell than we expected—there generally is out here—and once again it is a thrill to come out into this new environ. True; whether you view the sea, the coast and the weather from the deck of a 12,000 tonner or the cockpit of a bobbing dinghy they're the same . . . but from the latter they do appear to take a more personal interest in you!

Gulland rock is standing out grey and brown in the morning sunlight to the West. The Quies rocks off Trevose stand out black against the horizon; how far off do you think they are? Would you guess, without looking at the chart, a couple of miles? In fact the nearest of them is over four miles away! Distance judging at sea is very difficult because there is nothing in the foreground to which more distant objects may be related. One nearly always tends to underestimate, especially on a clear day like this. I would assess the windspeed here to be not more than ten knots—just under force four—and the sea conditions are fairly calm now we are clear of Stepper. We are running on a broad reach Starboard tack and our course from Stepper to Trevose is taking us close to Chimney and Gurley Rocks which are shown as having ten and nine feet over them respectively. Certainly they give us nothing to worry about this morning at high tide, but I will digress a moment to tell of an event which took place two years ago to illustrate how familiarity can breed a dangerous contempt.

I have been sailing these waters for some fifteen years and am well aware of the position of these two shallow patches, Gurley and Chimney. Never, until two years ago, had I seen even the heaviest of swell break on them. On that particular day there was a mountainous swell rolling in from the West but practically no wind at all. We were ghosting back along this coastline, five boats in line abreast with spinnakers set, each coaxing the last ounce of speed from the fickle wind. It was one of those hot drowsy summer afternoons when the whole world is trying to keep awake. Without warning we all heard what sounded like a fast jet plane approaching. Everyone was alerted for the volume of sound was frightening. It was no jet. Close astern of the boats was a seething mass of white foam but what was more horrific was the fact that we were viewing it momentarily from the top of a hill looking down into the trough of a monumentally large swell. This one freak swell had been just high enough to collapse on Gurley rock. If it had arrived a few minutes earlier perhaps all the boats would have been swamped. It was near to Low Water Springs, and we all ought to have known better than sail across such a dangerously shallow patch. It taught me a lesson I shall never forget: the sheer size of that breaker—and there was only that one—against the oily calm all around was one of the most shocking sights I have ever seen at sea. But today there is not the least chance of that happening.

## CONDITIONS ROUND HEADLANDS AND BENEATH CLIFFS

The Pilot tells us that there is a passage five cables wide between the Easternmost Quies rock and a conspicuous rock called the Bull just off Dinas Head. It further states that the channel should never be used except in case of necessity and it is very sound advice, applying to any headland where shallow channels and offlying rocks extend the headland to seaward. We gave this some thought in Chapter Two when dealing with the flow of a tidal stream along a coast, and here I propose taking you, with very little stream running, through one of these 'races'. You will appreciate that billions of tons of water which is some six hundred times denser than air, do not take kindly to suddenly being squeezed out around these headlands when flowing along the coast. The surface conditions up to two and more miles off can become quite alarmingly disturbed in the process. Where, as in this case, there are some really large rock masses amounting almost to small islands just seaward of the headland you may be certain there will be a violent sluice of water between them at full run of the tidal stream. Until you have actually gone through one of these races you cannot appreciate the effect they can have on a small boat. I know this area of coast very well: it is my home ground, so I know the conditions which will exist between the Bull and the Quies by the time we arrive there in about three-quarters of an hour. The tide will not yet be running very strongly but the effect will still be quite appreciable and I want to empha-size that we only take this passage because I have local knowledge. Were it not so it would be stupid to go against the advice of the Pilot.

As we approach the cliffs up here to weather of the head East-ward of Trevose, do you detect a change in the surface condi-tions? Though the wind has not appreciably altered in strength the sea is becoming more disturbed. It's almost as if somebody over there under the cliffs were violently agitating the surface and we are just entering the fringe of the disturbed area. In fact this is almost exactly what is happening: the waves running down from the North East are being baulked by the cliffs of the head-land. Their forward motion is stopped abruptly by the cliff face which sets up a contra wave-motion in the opposite direction back from the cliffs almost like the reflection of light from a mirror. The angle of incidence, just as light off a mirror, equals the angle of reflection, and the 'bounce' back of the waves sets up a very confused surface condition unlike anything one meets out in open water. It's impossible to orientate the boat so as to deal with it and one can get very wet by the odd peak slopping inboard . . . not a bit conducive to bird-watching!

This morning the conditions are not violent enough to worry about and I mention it simply because it is worth remembering if anything of a sea is running and may be closely linked with another phenomenon. You will realise that with an onshore wind, a cliff face will cause the wind to rise as it blows from sea to land. It does not blow vertically up the cliff face but more often forms a wedge of 'dead' air sloping from the top of the cliff down to sea level as illustrated in Figure 45.

The point is that in a small boat one can often be spanking

NOT A BIT CONDUCIVE TO BIRD-WATCHING!

along in a good breeze and get into this wedge of dead air which will cover that very area where the wave reflection is most marked. You find yourself becalmed just when you need the wind to get clear of the disturbed water, and it is not the best of conditions to start shipping oars. Have you ever tried rowing a boat rolling through perhaps 30°?

*Figure 45*

*Wedge of 'dead' air to weather of a cliff with confused water at the cliff foot.*

We will keep at least one and a half cables (300 yards) off those cliffs as we round the headland . . . we can see the Bull coming open of Trevose now, so Dinas Head will be appearing shortly. So far, apart from the slight choppiness of the water just mentioned, there has been nothing much to remark on. The wind has become a little fickle but one cannot expect anything else so close to a high shoreline but now as we approach the head itself I want you to take careful note of our speed over the bottom. This is not easy, for a correct assessment of speed over the bottom (as opposed to speed through the water) takes a lot of experience. It is gained by watching two marks ashore—you watch one near mark in relation to another some distance behind it. As you move so these marks will change their position relative to one another, and it is this rate of change relative to each other that gives you an indication of your own speed over the bottom. Of course the distance you are away from the marks has a great effect on this rate of change: the closer you are to the near mark, the faster it

will appear to move in relation to the far mark. If both of them
are a long way from you, with only a short distance separating
them they become virtually useless for speed assessment except
over a long period of time during which you may cover many
miles. But for this close inshore sailing, if you keep your eyes
about you, any local eddies or contra-running tidal streams can
be detected fairly quickly by this means. Try to make an assessment of our speed as we enter this channel between the Bull and
the Quies, noting what happens as we go through. Now we are
approaching the narrows, and do you detect that we have slowed
slightly just up-tide of the pass? Look at the water ahead; it
almost appears to be boiling silently and now watch the shore
carefully . . . we are already speeding up and in fact are in a
veritable mill race which is making steering very difficult. There
is no wind at all now—we are close under the lee of Trevose, but
the whirlpools are throwing the boat about, and remember this
is before the tidal stream has really begun to run strongly down
the coast. The Tidal Atlas predicts the rate as being just under
one knot out there a few miles off the head, but my estimation is
that here on the headland it is rushing through at a very disturbed
four knots and probably more. You may imagine what this area
is like at the full strength of half-tide with a Westerly wind
spanking against the ebb! We would have a very rough ride, and
would be well advised to give this particular headland and its
offlying rocks a good mile and a half clearance.

At the moment we are still feeling the lee of Dinas and Trevose
behind it but it won't be long before we break free of the wind
shadow, though for a while we can expect an eddy or two for it
will certainly be swirling around so close inshore.

## KEEPING ON THE TRACK LINE

It is from this point that we laid off our trackline on the chart
before leaving, and we now have before us some 26 miles of
exposed coastline, much of it high cliffs. In these circumstances
we shall be wise not to sail close inshore where we would certainly find variable wind effects under the lee. Since St Ives is the
target we shall do better to press on straight down our track line.
We know that to be 226° (C) so I am steadying her up just past
the 225° graduation on my steering compass. Wind and tide

being right behind us there is no appreciable set from the tide or drift due to wind for which we must allow. You will notice that we are now filling on a broad reach Port tack after that slight alteration of course.

We can see a very prominent headland almost due South which is certainly Park Head. Beyond that things get a bit difficult to identify and although we can see the coastline clearly it is impossible to pick out Towan Head with certainty, seven and a half miles from us. The farthest this track line takes us offshore is four miles, when halfway across Watergate Bay, and we are not the least bit worried about Medusa rock at a depth of nine fathoms down there. We are far more likely, by sticking to this track line, to get full advantage of the tidal stream. Close inshore we would experience back eddies and a general slackening of the rate. As it is we are bound to feel a 'set in' to Watergate Bay on the first leg of this stretch until we are somewhere off Mawganporth. After that we can expect to be 'set out' again to seaward as the ebb stream sweeps round the Southern end of Watergate Bay, but we shall not know exactly how much these factors are affecting us unless we fix our position and it will be wise to do this at least once every hour, or as opportunity occurs. Although we are perfectly well aware of our position at the moment, remember we have a long stretch ahead of us and visibility can easily change; if we should lose contact with the land it is imperative to know where we are in relation to that track line.

The time was 0905 when abeam of Dinas Head and it is close on 0930 now. A 'fix' on Dinas and Park Heads will give us a good cross cut of nearly a right angle. Park Head bears 135° by hand-bearing compass, and Dinas Head 046° (C). Plot that on the chart. My plot puts us about four cables inshore of our track line already, which confirms our expectations of a 'set in' to the bay, but there is not much point in our altering course for we shall certainly pick up the 'set out' off Newquay. Four miles offshore may not appear to be much when considering it at home, but out here we have to remember that it represents about one hour in time should we wish to beach the boat. In that hour the weather could quite easily deteriorate enough to preclude any thought of landing safely on the exposed beaches. I don't want to rub this in too much, but it is just because of this type of risk that one should plan the cruise in every detail with particular attention to the weather forecast.

Our very low height of eye above sea-level gives us a horizon which is about three to four miles away, and the shore seems a devil of a long way off. Dinas Head, which is already about three miles astern is still clearly visible but you will notice that the waterline below the head is completely straight which indicates that the foot of those cliffs is beneath our horizon. The weather remains fine and at this rate we shall certainly not be putting into Newquay.

ASPECTS OF THE COAST; WEATHER AND LIGHT EFFECTS

Worth noting here is the different appearance of even a well known coastline in varying conditions of weather and light. You noticed this morning how the cliffs between Stepper and Trevose looked black and ominous while Gulland and Newland rocks were bathed in brilliant sunlight. Had we been looking at this coast in the evening it would have taken on a quite different aspect. The cliffs, being in the sunlight, would have appeared less ominous and more indented. Valleys would have been thrown into sharp contrast by shadow, but any small offlying rocks would probably have been impossible to discern since they would tend to merge with the same coloured background.

In hazy weather a minor headland of no navigational value can appear to stand out strongly from a coastline when viewed obliquely, simply because a really prominent headland beyond, for which you may be looking, is not easily visible through haze. It is very easy when navigating to assume that a headland which materialises out of the mist is the one you are expecting, when in point of fact it's nothing of the sort, but something you did not even note from inspection of the chart. In clear visibility when one face of a promontory is in shadow while the coast behind is bathed in sunlight, the shadowed headland may stand out clearly even though a more prominent head beyond is unidentifiable as such because it is at a different angle with the light.

Size of offlying rocks when viewed from different positions and in different light can be most misleading. At a distance the Quies back there appeared to lie well off Dinas Head, and as large as islands. But as we passed through the channel it almost seemed one could leap from one to the other, and they appeared to have shrunk in size!

Though we cannot yet identify the end of Towan Head due to it merging with the land behind, I feel sure that is Newquay down there due South with the haze lying above it, in which case that must be Kelsey Head beyond with 'the Chick' just off it: you can see the Chick on the chart—it's that rock just North West of Kelsey. We will find out what Kelsey Head should bear from us by taking a fix now on Dinas and Park Heads. You plot the bearings: Dinas 032° (C), Park 082° (C). It's not the best of crosscuts because the angle is only fifty degrees between the two heads, but it will do. It puts us just to the East of that fifteen fathom sounding: note it in the log and put the time (0945) against the 'fix' on the chart. From that position on the chart give me a compass bearing to the Chick. According to my hand-bearing compass it is somewhere between 210° and 220°—the card is a bit unsteady so we must take the mean of 215°. You say the Chick should bear 219° by compass? Then that is certainly Kelsey Head down there and we are about a mile inshore of our track line, so there is a stronger 'set in' here than we estimated. We will alter course ten degrees to starboard and try to keep her steady on 236° (C) until we get back on station.

The wind, though remaining steady from the North East, has certainly eased in the last half hour, and clearly we must press on for St Ives. You will see there are a couple of wrecks charted ahead (marked on the chart by a horizontal line with three verticals crossing it, surrounded by a pecked circle) and note that their position is only approximate, which fact is indicated by the letters (P.A.) adjacent. They need not worry us, being in seventeen fathoms depth!

The important thing is to check when we are back on the track line, so at 1030 we will take another 'fix' and this time we will choose three objects ashore to eliminate any chance of error. Make a note in the log: Towan Head bears 135° (C), the Chick bears 186° (C) and Park Head bears 064° (C). Plot that and give me the Latitude and Longitude of the 'fix'. According to my plot it puts us in position 50° 26'.9 N., 05° 09'.0 W. I see the three-point bearing gave a small cocked hat and I hope the latitude and longitude you noted was taken from the centre of that triangle.

So we are now a mere three cables East of our track line again, and evidently we are being helped to seaward by that set out of the bay, so our ten degree alteration of course three-quarters of an hour ago will be too great from now on: bring her back on to 230° by compass and we'll have a bite to eat.

Our next point for thought is whether to pass inside Godrevy Island or to seaward of the Stones. The time is now 1330 and it is therefore Low Water, and what is more the wind is falling very light so if we are to use the last of the South Westerly flowing tidal stream it looks as if we shall have to proceed under power. I hope you will agree that it would be stupid to persist in trying to sail and by so doing meet the adverse tide before we reach St Ives. In any case, we will make the decision now to pass through the channel between the island and Godrevy Point, for although the Pilot tells us the depth in this channel is a mere ten feet, there is no large swell running and it will be quite safe. But understand that if we were having to beat against a South Westerly, or if there were any real swell, we would choose to pass North of the Stones whistle buoy, for this channel is too narrow to allow any safe tacking; there is foul ground off Godrevy Point.

Apart from a slight turbulence as we spew between shore and the island there will be nothing to worry about, and we shall have full control under power. After that we shall have only three and a quarter miles across St Ives Bay to make the harbour. We have been exceptionally lucky on this first leg of the trip by having a following wind and a calm sea; it has given us a chance to navigate with accuracy but it would not have been the case had we been meeting a head wind. Any sort of chartwork such as we have been doing would have been impossible.

The final decision we have to make is whether to enter St Ives and take the bottom during the night, or to remain at anchor just off the entrance and clear of it in sufficient depth to keep the boat afloat. The important thing to remember in this latter case is to ensure that at Low Water we shall still have sufficient depth under us to preclude the possibility of being inside any breaking waves should a swell or sea start running. It is all very well to calculate that one still has three feet of water beneath the keel at Low Water but if a swell builds up during the night and breakers start tumbling fifty yards seaward not only will you probably be swamped, but the hull will probably be stove-in on the seabed in the troughs!

ENTERING HARBOUR

Low Water at St Ives was a quarter of an hour ago at 1330 so the tide will start to rise now. But it is Springs, and probably we shall not yet be able to get inside the piers. Our problem is to arrange our position in harbour so that we are afloat by the time we propose leaving (weather permitting) tomorrow morning. First then: at what time should we aim to leave St Ives? It depends on the tides, and from the Atlas we see that at 0800 tomorrow there will be about half a knot running North East up this coast. By 0900 it has started to flow South West down the coast, and by 1000 it is flowing quite strongly at about two knots in a Southerly direction to sweep down South of Lands End and up the English Channel.

By 1100 it is flowing even more strongly round Land's End in excess of two knots and much the same conditions obtain West of Lands End at 1200, but by this time the stream has ceased to flow Eastward up the Channel and has started flowing South South West out of the Channel entrance. By 1300 this general South Westerly trend has increased in strength but it is evident that the strength of the tidal stream in Mounts Bay area is nothing like that flow out there fifty miles offshore. This is good for us: if we aim to sail at 0800 in the morning we shall pick up the favourable stream by 0900 down by Gurnard's Head. If the wind holds fair we can, under sail, be in the region of Longships Lighthouse at 1200 and still carrying a Southerly stream with us.

By 1300 we could be passing the Runnel Stone with a very slight adverse tide, and I'm afraid we shall have to stem this adverse tide until we put into Mousehole or Newlyn which will be the first ports affording real shelter on this second day of the trip. So from this bit of thinking it is evident that it really does not matter where we berth in St Ives because we shall be afloat at High Water tomorrow morning. What *is* important to note is that the Tide Tables indicate that High Water in the morning is about one foot less in height than High Tide tonight. We must therefore take the bottom tonight about one hour *after* High

Water to ensure that we shall float tomorrow: no sense in making work for ourselves!

That being the case we can have the afternoon ashore in St Ives, leaving her anchored at the entrance until this evening when she can be put on the beach well inside the piers. Our first duty now is to telephone back to Rock and report safe arrival, then seek out the Harbour Master for a berth tonight and tell him of our intentions for tomorrow. We will take the transistor ashore to get the 1757 Shipping forecast.

USE OF TRANSITS

The 0640 shipping forecast gives winds North to North East force five and moderating. We float in one hour. Force five is enough and to spare to be off an ironbound rocky coast in an open boat but it's direction and the fact that it is due to moderate tips the scale, plus the fact that at this moment it certainly isn't more than force three to four from the North East. Do you always feel like this in the morning? Put the kettle on while we plot today's track line on the chart. Start from a point half a mile true North of Carn Naun and join this to a position 50° 10′.0 N., 05° 43′.8 W. with a light pencil line. Transfer this line to the rose, using the lower rose—it's easier to reach. I make it 255° (C). From that position off Botallack Head it will be wise to lay off two alternative track lines down past the Longships. If visibility and sea conditions allow there is no reason why we should not take the inside channel between Longships and Land's End. If not we will go outside the lighthouse. Plot a track line therefore to take us from that last position off Botallack Head straight down through the inside channel and make it 8 miles along. My plotting makes that line 188° (C). From the same starting point lay off another 'seaward' track line to a position 1½ miles due West (True) of Longships lighthouse. From my chart that gives me 210° (C) for a distance of 6½ miles. Join that position to the Southern end of our 'inside' track line and extend it on to a position eight cables (0′.8) due South (True) of the Runnel Stone buoy. That gives us a track line 5½ miles in length, 140° by compass. Do you agree?

From Runnel Stone we might as well lay off a track line to a point due East (True) of Tater-du lighthouse just up the coast.

Plot it 070° (C) with a length of 5½ miles and that will take us to a position just off Tater-du from which we can steer 022° (C) until off the entrance to Mousehole with St Clement's Isle close on the starboard bow.

Note down those track lines with their lengths on a piece of paper which you can keep in your pocket; we shall be trying to keep to them, and we already know the tidal stream situation for today. If I tell you, reader, that on the day in question High Water at Devonport was at 0830 you might like to check the tidal stream situation at 0800, 1000 and 1200 in positions 'N', 'F', 'E' and 'D' diamonds on the chart to see if they more or less agree with our calculations of yesterday.

Have a cup of tea. There is one thing which concerns me more than anything else on today's passage—that race off Pendeen and Botallack Head. If you think I am going to take you through this one for the experience . . . Ha Ha for China! I have been slap through the middle of it in a Spring ebb tide with a strong South Wester aboard my forty foot yacht and we just about stood on our capsules. All the water in the entrance to the Bristol Channel elbows its way round this knuckle of the Cornish Peninsula on the ebb—you can see it on the Tidal Atlas—and it is then no place to be in an open boat. Even though the wind this morning is with the stream, we still have a Spring ebb behind us down this stretch which will be causing a deal of turbulence in that area. It is imperative that we keep on, or to seaward of that track line. As for creeping close inshore to pass inside the race, it would be foolish indeed for we would have to hug a rocky, cliffbound and altogether inhospitable shoreline with no guarantee that the sluice of tide would not take charge of the boat under the lee of the cliffs.

The time is 0800 with a fresh North Easter, so we will motor from the beach and get all sail on her as we make up to weather of the harbour entrance, then beat out on starboard tack to round the Island at St Ives Head. You may be sure that there will be a bit of sea running out there with the wind against the last of the North East flowing stream—in fact we can see it now, a typical 'wind against tide' sea; short, steep and wetting. We had better don oilskins as well as our buoyancy aids, and stow that chart away otherwise it'll be papier mâché. Just have a final check on that forward hatch: is it properly secured? We are going to have a blustery run to start with, but St Mawgan 'Met' confirm that the pattern today will almost certainly follow that of yesterday, the wind easing as the day gets older. If it were not so we would have stayed in St Ives.

Each time I find myself off the open coast in brisk conditions I realise that the line between enjoyment, excitement, and stark colliwobbles is very thin. The sea is so overwhelmingly vast, the coast so blindly indifferent, and the boat so pathetically small. This feeling does not arise from any lack of confidence in the boat or in my own ability: it comes simply from an understanding that we are being tolerated out here, and one unpredictable change in the weather could easily mean a hard and dangerous fight back to the nearest refuge. Our lives can depend on an accurate assessment of the situation, and making the right decisions. If that assessment and those decisions have been wrong, it's no use crying to the sea not to be cruel; her ears are already full of salt water and she won't hear.

This morning it's exciting as we free off round the Island to start our run down the coast. We are surfing occasionally on the face of the following seas which makes steering difficult. Waves tend to slap up under the counter and lift the stern sideways, with the attendant risk of broaching. If not handled properly that could, in these conditions result in the lee gunwale going under, most particularly if we had forgotten to raise the centre-plate because the plate would present lateral resistance.

Get the mizzen sail off her—in fact unship the mizzen mast and stow the lot along the side-deck to weather. Pressure on that sail right aft was increasing the tendency to broach. Without it all the pressure is forward of the rudder and centreplate (the latter is one quarter down) and she rides much more easily. If the seas get any worse we shall have to reef the main.

In the open sea one should avoid at all cost the chance of a continuous 'surf' down the front of a steep wave. It is one thing to have a helping slide occasionally as we are at the moment, but quite another to allow her to take the bit between her teeth and go all the way with a wave. If the latter happens she is almost bound to broach sooner or later, and meanwhile if the crests are tumbling she may easily be 'pooped'. This is when the crest, travelling at the same speed as the boat herself, continues to pour in over the stern until she is swamped. It was for this reason that the early sailing ships which could only sail before the wind, had their sterns built up tremendously high. It kept the 'poop' deck high above the following sea.

The Lugger has a good stern for this point of sailing: I like her short counter that gives a good lift, but if we start surfing too much we shall have to reduce speed by reefing or, if that is not sufficient, we shall hand all sail and trail a couple of warps astern to slow her down and allow those crests to pass on their way, not hang about round the stern. However, we have not reached that stage yet, though we can certainly not attempt to take or plot any fixes. This does present problems, for while it is important to keep at least a mile and a half seaward of Botallack Head we do not want to get too far offshore in this freshening wind—and it is freshening from the North East—because having got past that race we may have to close the land a bit to gain some slight lee. We can see the lighthouse at Pendeen but it is impossible to get a vertical sextant angle on it in this merry-go-round. Somehow we have to rely entirely on visual aids. From a rough sight along the steering compass is is evident we are about North of the lighthouse; but how far North? Over the port quarter we can see Gurnards Head standing proud of the coast but what is alarming is that we cannot see Zennor Head behind it, though we can still see Carn Naun point back near St Ives. Take a quick look at the chart: if Zennor isn't open of Gurnard we must be South of our track line and heading perilously close to the outer fringes of that race. See Figure 46.

That quick visual check is worth a tanker load of oil to us because we are evidently making some leeway, running on the Starboard tack as we are, and I am going to bring her round on to the wind and beat on Starboard tack until we can see Zennor. You understand why I am making such a large alteration of course to effect something which could have been achieved by a comparatively small correction? It is because any point of sailing between this broad reach and a beat will mean we shall have to take wind and seas slap on the beam. Beyond a certain condition of the surface this can be an unhappy and potentially dangerous point of sailing. Better by far to let the bow take these seas. I am waiting for a lull just after a sea has passed beneath us for the opportunity to turn, and here we go . . . harden sheets and I am going to keep plenty of way on by sailing on a close reach. It would be an advantage to step the mizzen again now, but since we shall only be beating for a few minutes it is hardly worth the effort, and anyway we have enough sail on already in this wind.

Here comes Zennor open of Gurnards Head. The time is 0945 and in about five minutes I am going to bring her back on to the

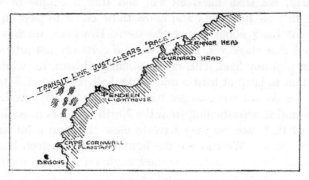

*Figure 46*

*Use of transit to clear offlying danger. Zennor Head was not open of Gurnards Head, indicating that our position was too close to the 'race' off Pendeen.*

run, keeping that transit well open until Pendeen lighthouse is due East by the steering compass. We are about a mile and a half offshore and lumpy as the sea may be out here you can be certain it is a deal worse to shoreward of us in that race. In fact you can clearly hear the seas breaking over there in the white water—a sort of continuous distant roar and I'm glad we're not in it.

The tide has swung in our favour by now and will be helping us; running with the wind as it now is, the sea in the last quarter of an hour has altered its character. There is little difference yet in the size of the waves, but there are fewer white horses which is a sure indication that wind and tide are starting to work together. Frankly, the conditions in the last half-hour have been marginal for safety off this bit of coast in an open boat, and I'm glad to see it easing. There is a slight swell rolling in from the

West, and as the tide starts strengthening this can be expected
to increase a little in height. One's inclination is to close the
shore having passed the race, to ensure a lee in case the wind
starts freshening again, but close inshore here is a very dangerous area. Inshore of the Brisons—those two vast rocks like small
islands about half a mile offshore—is particularly tricky, being
strewn with shallows and rocks. Indeed the coast round White-
sand Bay and Sennen Cove is a risky place to be unless one has
local knowledge.

We can see the Brisons just clear of Cape Cornwall to the
South. Visibility is good and we want to keep that transit of
Zennor and Gurnard just open until we get Lands End itself and
the Brisons in transit. Do you see why? That position off Pendeen
light from which we are due to alter course for the Longships is
exactly where the transit of Lands End and the Brisons cuts our
track line down from Carn Naun. When the two transit lines cut
(Zennor/Gurnards, Lands End/Brisons) we are due to alter
course for the Longships. It is useful to arrange alterations of
one's course at the intersection of transits like this: saves a lot of
messing about with instruments. But we are lucky in being able
to see Lands End, it's about six miles away.

The sea is calming down a lot now and the wind also has eased;
probably not more than force three at this moment. There is no
reason why we should not take the inner channel East of the
Longships lighthouse. Both transits are coming 'on' so note the
time (1045) and bring her round to 188° (C). We can reconstruct
the log when we get a chance later. Again today we are fortunate
in having the tidal stream parallel to our track line, so there has
been no need to allow for appreciable drift. We should by now
be experiencing a helping stream of about two knots which is
just as well, for it seems our motive power is deserting us . . . the
wind has dropped noticeably in the last quarter of an hour. This
is proving a more comfortable rounding of the land than we had
any right to expect!

FISHERMEN'S FLOATS

One of the greatest pests at sea when close inshore, and at the
same time one of the most useful signposts, is the system of floats
which fishermen put on their lobster pots. They are a menace

because unless a good lookout is being kept they can wrap themselves round one's centreboard, rudder, or worst of all the propeller. The pots lie on the bottom attached to a long thin floating
line which rises in a soft curve up to the surface where it may
float, when the stream is weak, for a long distance. At its end
there may be attached anything from two to six cork floats the
last one of which—at the extreme end of the line—has a short
cane stuck through it with a small flag on top. This cane and flag
is kept vertical by a small weight down at the foot beneath the
water. As the tidal stream starts to flow more strongly the line
itself pulls a little way under the water and often the first one or
two of the floats too will submerge a foot or so, leaving perhaps
the final float with the cane just on the surface.

It is only too easy to cross the line, perhaps some fifty feet
up-tide of the flag, wrapping the whole lot round the propeller
or what-have-you. At night they are the curse of the yachtsman.
On the other hand they are, as I say, one of the most useful signposts of the sea because they give one a very accurate indication
of the strength and direction of the tidal stream. By remembering
that the flag is always on the last float of the line, one merely has
to sight the flag and the line of floats to get a precise run of the
tide, and experience will enable you to assess the strength of the
stream by the degree in which the floats appear to be rushing
through the water. One tends to overestimate the strength of
tide: one knot will give the floats a splendid bow-wave. Figure 47
will make this clear.

The Brisons rock is just coming in transit with the flagstaff atop
Cape Cornwall so that tells us exactly where we are on the track
line. The time is 1145 so we have only made good three miles in
the last hour since altering course off the race. Since the wind is
now practically non existent most of that three miles has been
the effect of the tidal stream and remembering that we are now
approaching an area with many offlying rocks, we will hand all
sail and start the motor. Make a note of the time. Longships lighthouse is clearly visible to the South, and the swell which is running is making all the submerged rocks betray their presence by
an occasional breaker which leaves a splash of white foam on the
surface long after the swell has passed on. I much prefer these
conditions of low swell when there are submerged rocks around:

one gets ample warning. It's when there is no swell at all, but perhaps a choppy sea running, that you can inadvertently run a craft on a rock. With the white horses all around in those conditions you get no real warning.

*Figure 47*

*Fisherman's float attached to a lobster pot.*

*A good indication of speed and direction of the tidal stream.*

*A pest if you're not looking where you are going!*

Longships is abeam now to starboard. A vertical sextant angle reads 1° 20'.0 and since the light is marked as being 114 feet in height that puts us (with a bit of interpolation) eight cables East of the light—slap in the middle of the channel. That colossal rock, some eighty feet high just beneath the Lands End Hotel on top of the cliff is called the Armed Knight. Take a good look at it, and at the sea. The latter has that odd look again as though it were boiling and this is certainly due to turbulence over the very rocky bottom. It is in fact what makes this a most dangerous area when there is any sea and swell running. The water round this

Westernmost tip of the land can be hellish and only a fool would
venture here in doubtful weather with a dayboat.

### BACK EDDIES AND TELLTALE SPUME

But have you noticed that the transit of the Armed Knight and
the hotel on shore has not altered this last minute or so? Yet we
are doing a good four knots through the water! You've guessed
it: we are sitting in a strong back-eddy here. We may be moving
toward or away from that rock—it's hard to tell—but for sure we
are not moving past it. Give her more power to break through.
The Tidal Atlas may predict a maximum of two knots flow off
Lands End, but right close in to shore it is certainly more than
that in strength—and variable in direction. Remember this. It is
only what one might expect but it can catch you out badly.

Before we leave these massive offlying rocks around the Longships reef let us take a good look at them, stuck as they are in a
strong tideway. Where a rock breaks surface in a tidal stream
the water in its immediate locality tends to behave much as it
does round the hull of a large ship. In the former case the water
is flowing past the rock; in the latter of course the ship is pushing
through the water but relative to each other there is little difference. True, a rock is attached to the bottom and this results in a
completely different underwater activity, but at the surface the
flow behaves in much the same manner. It separates on the up-
stream side, flows down either side and circles round in eddies
on the downstream side much as it will do under the stern of a
large ship. The slightest swell, breaking as it will on the rock,
leaves a trail of foam and spume down either side of the islet,
and this will tend to follow the contours of the turbulence down
stream from the rock or island. Looked at from above, you will
often see what appears to be a wake downstream of any islet, and
the spume which is carried down by the flow of water tends to
accumulate along the junction where one body of water, moving
at a certain rate, meets another body of water which is moving
at a different rate. Long lines and eddies of spume form on the
surface and this can be very misleading for it gives the same
effect as those indications of shallow submerged rocks we were
discussing earlier. No doubt you have sometimes stood on a high
point of land and remarked on a continuous line of white foam

floating idly on the surface well clear of the shore. The photo on the jacket of this book is a good illustration of this. You may be sure that the line of spume one can see which so closely follows the contour of the shore will mark the line where a weak tidal stream starts to run. To shoreward of the spume—where my boat is—will be the static water. Frequently you can detect eddies and small whirlpools at this junction of the two different speeds of flow where the spume collects.

But we must press on now under power, and since we have complete control of the boat and are not relying on a fickle wind we will ignore our trackline and motor close inshore along this Southerly tip of the land. So long as we keep a wary lookout we can 'rock hop' under these ideal conditions and pass inside the Runnel Stone. Allowing for a swim on the way we should be off Mousehole by 1430. I have been round Lands End many times, and through this inner channel twice before but never remember seeing it so calm and oily as this. We are not alone either: over there to seaward, do you see those two black fins? One looks stationary while the other flaps idly and they are all of ten feet apart, but they're part of the same fish! It is a basking shark and quite harmless but I have heard tales where these monsters have rubbed themselves against the keels of small boats, causing some consternation, so don't go trying to prod them with an oar; they might win. I'm told they eat nothing bigger than plankton, and almost believe it.

IN A TIDAL HARBOUR

Mousehole is one of the most pleasant little harbours on this South West coast. Protected from the open sea by two long quays, and St Clements Isle, a rocky outcrop due East, it is entered through a narrow opening between the ends of the quays which, in winter is sealed completely. This is effected by dropping horizontal baulks of timber into specially constructed guides at either side, and it stops the tremendous surge of swell raised by the winter gales from entering the harbour. At Spring tides it dries right out to the entrance, so forms a good example of a small tidal harbour which is used by fishing craft up to about sixteen and eighteen feet in length plus the odd pleasure boat which is able to take the bottom. The method of securing the boats is by a series of running moorings. A very heavy chain is run along the beach above High Water mark just at the foot of the town wall. To this is attached a series of blocks every twenty feet or so. An endless line is rove through each of these blocks down the beach into the deepest part of the harbour where it is rove through another block attached to a heavy sinker. The boats make fast bow and stern to these lines, often bringing their lines through the forward fairlead, round the samson post and out through the stern fairlead so that the line runs over the top of the boat. Having disembarked, the owner can then pull her on the endless rope back into deep water where she will remain afloat and may be pulled in at any time and at any state of tide except perhaps Low Water Springs. In Mousehole these lines run in profusion up the beach, and visiting craft will be acting with courtesy when mooring by ensuring that the boat does not foul these lines. The keel of a boat, while surging back and forth at the moment of taking the bottom on a falling tide, can easily cut these running moorings. Rope is expensive.

Of course immediately on arrival one reports to the Harbour Master to get his instructions on where to lie, and often there will be a running mooring not in use which may be offered. In the event of all the boats being on their moorings however it will fall to the visitor to make his own arrangements so as not to foul any of the other craft or their lines. Bearing in mind the dangerous exposed fluke of a Fisherman's anchor I propose to drop my stern anchor without the stock in position so that both flukes lie flat on the bottom. This has two advantages in such a situation. Apart from removing the risk of another boat impaling herself thereon, on a rising tide it will enable us to pull the boat back to the shoreline when we return after being away in Town. To be able to drag the stern anchor has certain advantages! We will hitch our bow anchor over the chain up the beach and put a bucket over the fluke to prevent accidents that end.

A word about taking the bottom. Obviously one should ensure that there are no sharply projecting stones that could go through the hull as she settles, and you may be sure that when she floats over one tide she will not settle in exactly the same spot, so it pays to clear the area all around. We are sleeping aboard this boat, and it is much more pleasant to remain on a level keel.

Without any support under the bilge keels she will lie to an angle of about 10° off the vertical which makes life awkward. But take care if using stones to chock the boat that they are removed as soon as she floats, otherwise they will be sure to go through the hull skin when next she settles! We overcame this danger by making two chocks of wood which kept her on an even keel when placed beneath the bilge keels. Both were attached by a stout piece of elastic to the gunwale. When wedged beneath the keels the elastic was under tension but as soon as the boat lifted on the tide during the night the chocks were pulled free from under the boat and floated clear while still being retained. It worked, and saved a lot of turning out at grim hours.

So there it is. It has been a good trip round and we must now report our arrival back to Rock. I hope it may serve to help you give proper thought to planning a cruise. The art lies in knowing when to go and when not to go. Of course as you do more of it you will take less chances because your experience will increase.

But sometimes, even after the most careful planning, the sea or the weather—or both—decide to give you a run for your money. It happens with the best of us and the next chapter is included to give you confidence when that first occasion comes your way. The first time is generally the worst, and when it happens you'll certainly wish you were back in the local pub. But if you handle it correctly you will have something to talk about for the rest of your life and it's worth every minute of it.

Afterwards.

# 8

# Caught Out

## FOG

More often than not there is due warning of this, and if one does decide to sail when there is fog in the offing those points of safe refuge on the passage should be surveyed with even greater attention, so that should visibility start to clamp down one can make for the safe place before losing visual contact.

This is one circumstance where a small boat has the advantage over a larger craft. One has such immediate control, being able to turn in a few yards away from any danger looming up such as rocks or the like, and since fog and rough water are more or less incompatible—wind necessary to knock up a sea soon clears away the fog—one usually has good warning of approaching danger by the sound of it. Low swell breaking on a rock can be heard a long way off in calm conditions.

The greatest hazard for a small boat in thick fog is that of being run down, and it is for this reason that I do advise a cruising man to carry a small radar reflector which may be hoisted by a halyard. My own experience with merchant shipping leaves me with nothing but apprehension concerning fog. I have been on the bridge of a merchant ship whose radar was out of action doing twelve knots on auto-pilot in moderate fog. At times no lookout was on duty either and I could not help wondering what would be the fate of any small craft which happened to be in the way! I am not saying that this is a frequent state of affairs aboard merchant ships, but it does happen, particularly on some of the small coasters. In addition, even though a good watch is being kept by radar, sometimes this fails to pick up really small boats despite their reflector. It is very unwise to take the attitude, 'My reflector's up there; I can carry on regardless.'

If you are caught in a shipping channel or any area of water where craft are still likely to be operating, make it your business to get out of it as quickly as possible and anchor well away from the channel. Soundings with the leadline are invaluable here; one can creep close inshore where no deep draught vessel could proceed, and lie at anchor safely until the fog clears.

Sounds become strangely affected in thick fog, and in the blanket of absolute stillness you may hear noises a great distance away which normally you might not notice, yet a sound quite close at hand is sometimes almost inaudible. It is caused by odd refraction of the sound waves through the varying densities of moisture-laden air, and can throw one's assessment of sound direction completely out. You have only to lie becalmed in a thick fog while listening to the diaphone of a local lighthouse to realise that it can appear to come from any direction and the more you concentrate the odder the illusion.

You simply *must not* get caught in fog off an ironbound coast such as that down which we have just sailed. It is one thing to hand all sail and wait for it to clear, but what of that tide? It can drift you at a couple of knots in among offlying rocks and the chance of anchoring effectively in twelve fathoms of water and more is remote in a dayboat.

As we have seen, the Collision Regulations state that a craft of less than 40 feet in length when under way shall make an efficient sound signal at intervals of not more than one minute. A small gas operated foghorn is one of the best means of doing so but these do not last indefinitely and one is tempted to just sit and listen carefully, taking the attitude that when a sound something like another boat is heard one can start to make the signal. The other chap is probably doing exactly the same thing—creeping stealthily along with engine stopped and a bit of way on, listening to the silence! Make a noise of some sort as prescribed; bell if anchored (and you have one) or horn if under way. But let them know you are there.

With the looming up of a fogbank it is usually possible to take a bearing on some selected point of refuge before it becomes lost to you. Head straight for it and note the compass course. Allow roughly for any tidal stream and then, if overtaken by the fog take soundings as you go in. Though you may land up in the

main sewer outlet instead of the harbour mouth, you'll not be too
far out in your landfall!

ROUGH SEAS

Through bad luck or sheer bad management you may, perhaps
once or twice in a lifetime (one tends to learn from this sort of
thing very quickly) get caught off an exposed coastline in a rising
wind and sea and a swell which precludes landing. If there is a
lee under some promontory or cliff then of course you should
make for it before conditions get too bad. Far better to be
snugged down under the lee of a cliff than swamped out in open
water. The danger here is if the wind swings to put you on a lee
shore!

In a small highspeed 'planing' powerboat one does not need
much of a sea to be in fairly serious trouble. As already stated in
Chapter Three the highspeed hull is just not shaped to cope with
the short, steep seas with breaking crests such as we are now
considering. In such a boat one will be in the awkward position
of not being able to maintain the designed operational speed (any
thought of 'planing' would be suicide) yet unable with safety to
ride out such seas at low speed. We have had thoughts on what
happens if there is a power failure—immediate swing of the bow
down wind which exposes the engine and low transom to the
crests. The only sensible thing in this event is to hold her head-to-
wind by whatever means available. Anchor if possible or, if not,
improvise a sea-anchor from the bow. Throw out anything which
will cause a drag in the water, inhibit the drift, and keep her
head-to-wind. After that it's up to you. Get the engine going
again and ease her gently into the waves taking them dead on
the nose if they are tumbling at the crest, then angling off again
to gain a bit more way toward one's destination. It is far safer in
such conditions to work one's way into the breaking seas rather
than across, or trying to run with them. Both the latter courses
would be risky in the sort of craft we have in mind here and the
real answer is just not to get caught out in this type of boat.

Low speed launches with conventional hulls will have a better
chance of surviving longer, being designed more to ride the seas.
The best policy is, again, to decide on the nearest refuge—
preferably to windward—and ease her gently into each breaker

so as to maintain speed but not so fast as to drive her bow under the wave or augment too much the already violent motion. If your place of refuge is to leeward and you are already of the opinion that to turn and run before the seas would be dangerous, the only safe action would be to put out a sea-anchor of some sort and allow the boat to drift slowly down wind while head-to-sea until roughly abeam of the safe area. She can then be gently eased across the wind and seas, edging crabwise into the safe water, having first recovered the sea-anchor of course. If one carries a small mizzen sail—and many of these traditional small powerboats do—this is a tremendous help for it assists in holding the boat head-to-wind and also inhibits the violent rolling.

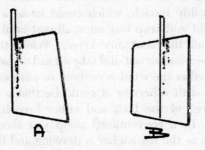

*Figure 48*

(A) *Normal rudder*
(B) *Balanced rudder*

Bear in mind however that any stern-way can be very punishing on a rudder if the blade is not balanced (see Figure 48). Some powercraft do have a balanced rudder, but balanced or unbalanced, it is much kinder on the mechanics of the whole assembly if the rudder blade is held centred while making stern way. In my lugger the rudder, although not balanced, is free to rotate through a full 360 degrees, so that when making stern way the blade may still trail.

If your boat is a double-ender (i.e. Norwegian stern) she will be better equipped for making a run down wind to safety, since the stern is built to part the following sea whereas a normal transom can slap badly. Transom hung rudders are particularly liable to be punished when running before breakers. Think 'rudder' at all times, and be as kind to this vital piece of equipment as possible: it may save your life.

In any form of sailing craft, by the time a rising wind and sea has developed to the state we envisage here, you will of course have reduced sail to the maximum compatible with maintaining steerage way. If refuge lies to windward, continue beating, easing the boat's bow gently up into the big waves, then freeing her off somewhat as opportunity permits so as to gain a reserve of momentum for the next big one. This takes great skill; if you head her up too early into a wave she may lose momentum to a point where the wave will stop her dead. This is dangerous because she is likely to fall off the wind violently with the next wave and possibly broach, which could mean a capsize. Keep the boat upright and keep way on at all cost until you decide it's pointless to sail the boat any longer. When that decision is reached get a sea-anchor out and take all sail off her immediately. No matter whether the wind is onshore or offshore, do what you can to reduce drift otherwise it could be that a breaking wave will take charge of the boat and either broach, surf, or even pitchpole her. In a conventional sloop you should unship the rudder as soon as the sea-anchor is drawing and then, if possible with safety, lower the mast to reduce windage and weight aloft. Keep your weight near the centre of the boat, low down and slightly toward the stern. I would advise bringing the centreplate (or centreboard) about threequarters up under this circumstance because to leave it right down does tend to give the bow a fulcrum when knocked sideways by a wave, most particularly if the boat has stern-way on. This can result in a broaching. A little 'plate' will serve to dampen down any violent rolling but offer negligible resistance laterally round which the boat could pivot. What is more, in the event of a capsize you will at least have the plate ready to pull out for the righting drill. It can be very awkward when that plate is completely housed! Unless your drift to leeward is taking you directly into sheltered water you have now reached a situation where distress signals could be used. You must make that decision after properly weighing up the actual situation and my only advice here is that it is better to use them and perhaps wish afterwards that you had not done so than to delay—and wish afterwards that you had! After that there is little you can do except bail so as to keep her dry. The more water you have slushing about in the bilges the slower will be the boat's responses and the less freeboard she will have. You will need the maximum of both!

With regard to running before a brisk wind with a following sea, one word of warning . . . do not gybe in order to change tacks unless you are very experienced. Round up, go about, and then bear away on the opposite tack avoiding a dead run so as to reduce the chance of an accidental gybe and the subsequent tendency to broach. If your refuge lies down wind and conditions are building up to a point where further sailing is too hazardous you may do one of two things, depending on how bad the seas have become. Either hand all sail and run off under bare pole with rudder in use, trailing a couple of floating lines (or any spare lines you have aboard) to slow down your progress and reduce risk of surfing, or, if you dare not present your stern to the seas, drift back with your sea-anchor attached to the stem, rudder un-shipped. If you can manage to get within any sort of lee you can then get a rag of sail on her and work into calmer water, beach-ing as and when possible. If you have no shelter and a lee shore close behind you, get her mast down and when you have drifted into moderately shallow water heave your ground anchor over with the longest line available attached. Then pray.

Finally, if despite this you are still dragging back on to a beach (and you are lucky enough for it to be a beach and not rocks) just let her lie to that anchor and sea-anchor keeping her head into the breakers and when the first of the real surf begins to roar astern cast off that ground anchor, leaving the sea-anchor fast so that she stays head-to-sea even though swamped. The reason for casting off the ground anchor is simply that you do not want to delay any longer getting on to that beach astern, and she will drift much faster—even possibly surfing in on a big one—without the ground anchor which might get a secure hold just at the wrong moment! So long as the boat remains semi-buoyant hold on like grim death but do not lash yourself in because in the event of her rolling right over you may be crushed by being rolled under with her. Keep a cool head and a firm hold until the moment when you first feel the boat strike the bottom. Then, if the beach is sloping sharply leap as far ashore as possible and don't get dragged back in an undertow. If it is a very gradually sloping beach your boat will strike bottom well out from shore and it will be better to stay with her as long as possible. You may be sure that in the situation we envisage, if she is at all buoyant she will be drifting into shallower water all the time. Leave her only when you are certain you can get to dry land safely. The golden rule is to keep her head into the seas and stay with the boat. This is about all you can do, and you will be lucky if you have the opportunity afterwards to reflect on the idiocy of ever getting into such a mess!

### SEA-ANCHORS

We have put a lot of faith in this item of equipment, so a word or two on exactly how it works is advisable. A sea-anchor is intended to cause a drag in the water sufficient to keep a boat headed into the seas. It is important that the device does not hold *too* well otherwise the bow, by not being able to lift, may plunge

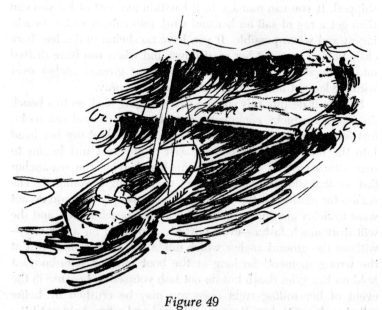

*Figure 49*

*Sail attached to spar forms an improvised sea-anchor*

through a big wave instead of over it. The sea-anchor must give just enough to let the bow lift, yet hold sufficiently to keep her head into the seas. Lots of things may be used as improvisations; a bucket on the end of a long line, or better still a sail while still attached to its boom or gaff. See Figure 49.

This latter has the added advantage of somewhat flattening the tumbling crests just before they reach the boat, but the warps (which are attached to the extremities of the spar as illustrated) are best led from either bow of the boat rather than the stem-head otherwise the whole paraphernalia gets twizzled.

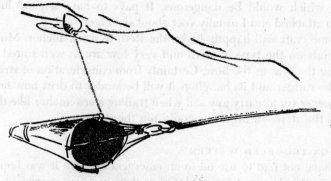

*Figure 50*

*The sea-anchor. One inch diameter at the mouth for every foot of boat.*

A proper sea-anchor consists of a rigid hoop to which is sewn a cone of stout canvas, open at the hoop end and the smaller end so as to allow a certain amount of water to flow through—rather like a parachute in air. See Figure 50.

The diameter of the mouth formed by the hoop should be roughly equal to one inch for every foot length of boat, and the length of the cone should be about two and a half times the diameter of the hoop. It is often recommended that a 'tripline' should be attached to the smaller end of the sea-anchor to facilitate hauling the device back aboard but from my experience this is not really practicable. The 'tripline' get fiendishly entangled with the anchor warp and becomes useless. In any case the size of the sea-anchors we are working with causes little difficulty when hauling them back aboard. These devices are worth carrying and you do not need to be in a storm for them to be of use. Often when jigging for fish out there I harden my mizzen sheet, hand the main and jib, and cast out my sea-anchor to slow down the rate of drift. I have a pound weight sewn into one side of the mouth against the hoop, and always attach a floating fender by a fathom of line to the opposite side of the hoop before casting it overboard. This ensures that the cone sinks below the surface but does not allow it to sink too far: you will appreciate that if the sea-anchor went too deep it would exert a downward pull on the bow which would be dangerous. It pays to have a good long warp attached and I usually veer about sixty feet.

Some craft will happily lie by the stern to a sea-anchor. Much depends on the type of stern and very few are as well suited to taking the seas as the bow. Certainly from consideration of strain on the rudder and its hangings it will be kinder to drift bow first, but *never* try to carry any sail when trailing a sea-anchor like this from the stern—a big wave could pin the stern under.

OIL ON TROUBLED WATERS

I have not had to use oil in an emergency where it was hoped to save the day, and I'm glad. Other than in a few special situations I have grave doubts if it would be much advantage. True, a very thin film of oil will do remarkable things to calm the white crests of tumbling waves, though it does little or nothing to reduce the size of the wave itself. The difficulty lies in effecting this calming exactly where you want it—where it will do you some good and continue to do so!

A boat in a strong wind will drift; regardless of whether she has a sea-anchor out or not she will drift appreciably. A film of oil will not . . . at least not nearly so fast as the boat. So when you distribute the oil from your boat, no matter how this be done, there results a splendid calming of the crests up to windward of you, and the effect gets farther to windward of you with every passing minute. If you put out a ground anchor in non-tidal waters the oil film will drift slowly to leeward with the surface movement of the water. If there is any tidal stream running you will say goodbye to it immediately.

One situation however where it would be of real value is where a rescue craft, equipped with oil, is in the offing. Oil spread on the water just to leeward of the stricken craft would give a breathing period during which the rescue craft could close the victim as the latter drifted through the oil and perhaps effect a transfer of crew by passing a lifeline.

Concerning the type of oil best for the job, I have found during tests that petrol mixed with oil, such as normal outboard motor fuel, spreads very quickly over a large area but soon becomes ineffective. Diesel fuel oil is a little slower to spread but remains effective longer, while lub-oil as used for the sumps of car engines coagulates into blobs on the surface at first then slowly spreads and remains effective longest of all. It would seem therefore that the thicker the oil, within limits, the more effective and long lasting the result. But whatever you use, put it close to leeward—then act fast.

### FEAR

This is a very real factor when thinking of safety at sea. We all have our thresholds of fear no matter in what field they operate, and it is a quite natural reaction to danger. Ashore it stimulates us to a heightened awareness and triggers off certain chemical reactions within us which are conducive to greater effort and quicker responses than would be normal. This can be advantageous; in some circumstances it can be lethal.

At sea fear works in much the same way, and it is all a matter of degree. Apprehension is acceptable—it may switch on a red light which persuades you to take a safe course of action where alternatives exist. Fear itself, which comes next up the scale toward panic, reduces your competence. Panic renders you quite useless and a hazard to all.

I cannot tell you where your fear threshold is in a boat, but you ought to know this yourself. Some people are afraid of the sea. To such people a quiet trip round the bay on a calm afternoon is a venture to be remembered. If the sea roughens up they will be afraid. It is easy to pour ridicule on such people, but it is very unfair. If that person who is afraid manages to keep a cool head in the face of the fear, then he or she is acting courageously and should be admired, not ridiculed. It is easy when you think you know all the answers to exhort people to 'keep cool', and is in fact very necessary that they should do so, for when real danger strikes the flame of panic can act faster and be a greater hazard than the original danger itself. But remember if panic starts it is vitally important that the one in charge should remain calm: example is perhaps the best of all ways to help others regain control of themselves.

There is a sure way of raising one's own fear threshold—in fact pushing it so far back that even dire emergency is viewed simply in terms of a disciplined query: 'What is the best course of action now?' Experience is the key. Find out where your own fear threshold lies by noting your first feeling of turning jelloid around the knees, then deliberately and coolly deal with the situation. The oftener this happens the less you will turn jelloid because it is the *unknown* which is feared. Experience is the best form of training.

Consider that chap we left back in Chapter Four clinging to a couple of airbags while his boat was pulverised on the rocks. If that was his first trip to sea the chances are (if he has any chances) he'll take to gardening in the heart of England, and by-pass the village duckpond.

If, on the other hand, he happened to be an experienced surfer who knew the way of a wave, lived with them and got his 'kicks' from them, then in such a situation he might merely be doing a mental calculation as to the efficacy of his boat's insurance policy. He would be more likely to survive than our potential gardener.

The point is, because you can sail a dinghy or drive a power-boat across a lake, do not think that you can with the same equanimity take the boat along an exposed coastline. Get to it in easy stages first: build up the experience gradually.

Finally, reject the thought that at the far end of this sliding scale of experience and competence lies foolhardiness. That is another track line altogether: experience has nothing to do with it. The chap who will act in a foolhardy manner when in charge of a boat does not do so because he is full of experience and very competent. He does so because he is that sort of chap. He would act similarly on a bowling green.

Steer clear of him at sea.

# Index